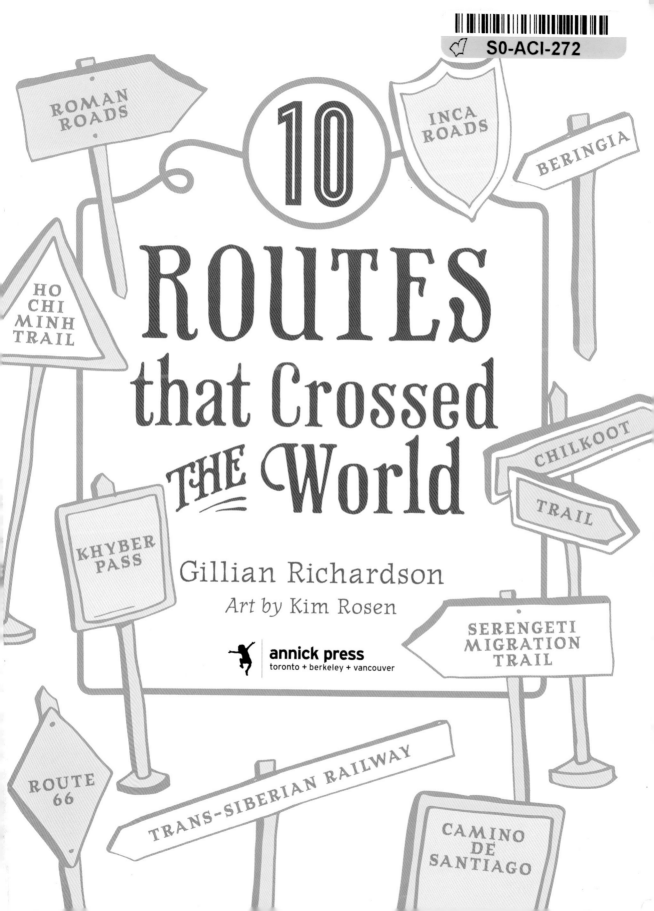

10 ROUTES that Crossed THE World

ROMAN ROADS

INCA ROADS

BERINGIA

HO CHI MINH TRAIL

CHILKOOT TRAIL

KHYBER PASS

SERENGETI MIGRATION TRAIL

ROUTE 66

TRANS-SIBERIAN RAILWAY

CAMINO DE SANTIAGO

Gillian Richardson

Art by Kim Rosen

annick press
toronto + berkeley + vancouver

To the adventurous who blaze trails, and the curious who follow them—G.R.

ANNICK PRESS LTD.

Cataloging in Publication

Richardson, Gillian, author
10 routes that crossed the world / Gillian Richardson ; art by Kim Rosen.

Includes bibliographical references and index.
Issued in print and electronic formats.
ISBN 978-1-55451-876-0 (hardback).–ISBN 978-1-55451-875-3 (paperback).–
ISBN 978-1-55451-877-7 (html).–ISBN 978-1-55451-878-4 (pdf)

1. Voyages and travels—History—Juvenile literature. 2. Travel—History—Juvenile literature. 3. Migrations of nations—Juvenile literature. 4. Emigration and immigration—Juvenile literature. 5. Trails—Juvenile literature. 6. Roads—Juvenile literature. 7. Mountain passes—Juvenile literature. I. Rosen, Kim, 1978–, illustrator II. Title. III. Title: Ten routes that crossed the world.

G175.R53 2017   j910.9   C2016-906712-2   C2016-906713-0

Published in the U.S.A. by Annick Press (U.S.) Ltd.
Distributed in Canada by University of Toronto Press.
Distributed in the U.S.A. by Publishers Group West.
Printed in China
Visit us at: www.annickpress.com
Visit Gillian Richardson at: www.books4kids.ca/gillian-richardson/
Visit Kim Rosen at: www.kimrosen.com
Also available in e-book format.
Please visit www.annickpress.com/ebooks.html for more details. Or scan

CONTENTS

Introduction

From ancient times to modern days, people have laid trails across the land. If we follow their footsteps along these routes, we find stories of migrations, discoveries, wars, and the settling of new countries. They tell us of tests of faith and dreams for the future. The journeys may be long or short, but you'll be amazed by how far they've reached, the traces they've left, and the lives they've changed.

The story of how the first humans reached North America is still uncertain because solid evidence is tough to find. Ice Age melting flooded the earliest possible route from Asia across BERINGIA. But other civilizations did leave visible clues in the remains of their roads. The conquering Roman Empire ruled Britain for over 400 years, due chiefly to their well-built road system. You can still travel parts of these ROMAN ROADS today. Across the world, in 16th-century South America, an ancient culture left similar proof of a well-organized realm: INCA ROADS were a marvel of engineering in a mountainous setting. Another well-used trail needed no construction: the feet of millions of animals blazed a migration route across Tanzania's SERENGETI plains, followed closely by aboriginal people whose lives are still linked to this seasonal movement.

Routes have offered promises to people through the ages. Since the ninth century, pilgrims have quietly hiked the CAMINO DE SANTIAGO in northern Spain to strengthen their faith. In the late 1800s, thousands rushed to conquer the short but treacherous CHILKOOT TRAIL in Alaska in hopes of finding the gold they'd chosen to worship. Around the same time, the TRANS-SIBERIAN RAILWAY—the world's longest railway line—opened Russia's vast undeveloped lands to new settlement and commercial potential. Later, amid tough economic times in the 1930s, Americans flocked west on a new road, **ROUTE 66,** eager for the end of the Great Depression.

Two ancient routes in Asia have seen turmoil with far-reaching impacts. The **KHYBER PASS** between Afghanistan and Pakistan, historically a route for invaders, has a dangerous reputation in today's political scene. The **HO CHI MINH TRAIL**, a series of jungle trading pathways, became known instead for devastation and death during a 20th-century war.

These 10 routes, at different times and in different places, have pointed the way to discovery, to wealth, and even to disaster. Shoulder your backpack, check your map, and set off through these stories of fascinating journeys.

A bridge across the Kama River, on the Trans-Siberian Railway

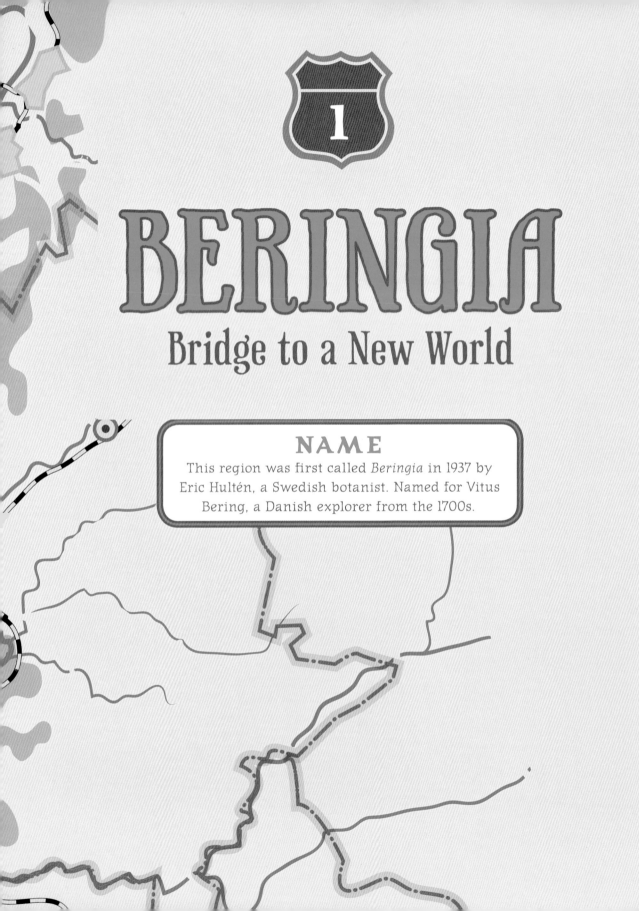

1

BERINGIA

Bridge to a New World

NAME

This region was first called *Beringia* in 1937 by Eric Hultén, a Swedish botanist. Named for Vitus Bering, a Danish explorer from the 1700s.

DESCRIPTION

The land mass of Beringia extended up to 1,810 kilometers (1,125 miles) from north to south—the distance from Seattle to Los Angeles. It reached from northeast Siberia all the way to Alaska, and as far east as the Mackenzie River near the Yukon–Northwest Territories border. Think of it as stretching over twice the size of Texas.

AGE

The land bridge appeared 20,000 years ago, at the peak of the Ice Age, when water froze in glaciers, causing sea levels to drop as much as 122 meters (400 feet).

BERING STRAIT

ASIA   ALASKA

PACIFIC OCEAN

CLAIM TO FAME

The central part of Beringia, called the Bering Land Bridge, is widely believed to be the land route between Asia and Alaska that allowed early people to migrate into North America at least 15,000 years ago.

WHO USES IT NOW?

The land that once linked the continents now lies underwater in the Bering Strait. But land on the Alaska side has been protected as the Bering Land Bridge National Preserve, and it's inhabited by wildlife and used by hunters, fishers, and other visitors.

Alaska, 2016

Leslie stares at the curved, whitish object that an archaeologist is dusting free of sand. He tells the people standing around the edge of the dig site that it is likely a prehistoric mammoth rib. Other bones are lined up on the ground, possibly more pieces of the huge creature that walked here 15,000 years ago during the Ice Age. Even more amazing for Leslie is that she's just stepped along an ancient trail that prehistoric people might have used when they were the first to walk this land. Was this how astronauts felt when they landed on the moon?

Yesterday, Leslie and her dad flew here in a small plane from the city of Nome, Alaska, to visit a remote part of the Bering Land Bridge National Preserve. As they cruised above the coastline, Leslie peered through the clouds across the Bering Strait to Russia—close enough that if there'd been a highway they could have driven there in an hour. Leslie tried hard to imagine what it must have looked like during the Ice Age, when the sea level was much lower, leaving the strait high and dry for humans to cross into North America.

The pilot had then veered east, away from the coast, flying over the tundra, where permafrost never really thaws in the short arctic summer. Leslie saw grasses, brightly colored wildflowers, low-growing shrubs, and small ponds. Her dad said they might spot moose or caribou, or even brown bears and wolves. Before the land bridge got covered by rising water, some of those animals crossed from one continent to another, too.

Leslie and her dad will spend three days in the National Preserve staying in a bunkhouse. She's looking forward to soaking in the Serpentine Hot Springs pool after today's hike back from the dig site, and trying to imagine what treasures the scientists might uncover tomorrow.

Cape Espenberg, at the edge of what used to be the Bering Land Bridge

The Story of Beringia

THE EARTH'S GLACIERS ARE MELTING! You've probably seen photos comparing the glaciers of years ago with today's much smaller ice sheets. Scientists believe a general warming of Earth's climate is causing this change. They point to rising sea levels—around 20 centimeters (8 inches) in the past 100 years—as evidence. About half of this extra water is coming from melting glaciers. If the trend continues, eventually low-lying shorelines will be flooded or submerged. We can study the problem helped by knowledge of what happened long ago.

If you can imagine it, once, a giant land mass off the northwest coast of North America stretched between Siberia and Alaska,

providing a route for people to cross between the two continents. But around 15,000 years ago, that land began to disappear beneath a sea of melted ice as global temperatures warmed. If you go there now, you can stand on the Alaskan shoreline and look west across the Bering Strait toward Russia. You'd need a boat to cross this channel joining the Arctic and Pacific Oceans, though it is fairly shallow—only about as deep as a 10-story building is high. This was once the Bering Land Bridge, only a small portion of the huge region called Beringia.

The mere existence of Beringia is fascinating to think about, but it's also exceptionally significant for understanding how humans came to settle in the Americas. Why is this particular place so important? Archaeologists believe the first humans to arrive in North America came from Asia by crossing Beringia before water cut off the route. José de Acosta, a Jesuit priest, first suggested this Asian origin theory in 1590, based on his observations while working with indigenous people in Mexico and Peru. It was an astonishing idea at the time, but by the 1930s enough clues had been found on the floor of the Bering Sea to convince scientists to consider it seriously. Decades of studying evidence such as bones and tools, combined with more recent discoveries from analyzing DNA—the material in our cells that carries genetic information about our heritage—are only now providing enlightening details. But the full picture is not yet clear, and the mystery of migration to North America may never be completely solved.

GLOBAL WARMING? BUT WE'RE IN AN ICE AGE!

The Earth has had at least five ice ages, or long-term cold periods. The most recent one began two million years ago, and it isn't over yet, as evidenced by permanent ice covering Antarctica, the Arctic, and Greenland (only a little melts in summer temperatures). But there's no need to rush for warm blankets. Ice ages have irregular warmer and colder spells, and we are in the middle of a warmer, or "interglacial," time right now. It began between 11,500 and 10,000 years ago. And it might last a long time yet because of global warming.

What Did Beringia Look Like?

STANDING IN BERINGIA 20,000 YEARS AGO, you would have been a tiny dot in an enormous land surrounded by ice, but with a climate dry enough to keep snow and ice from covering it. In the extremely cold northern parts of Beringia, few plants grew. Without food, no animals could live there, although they might have crossed the land during seasonal migration journeys. In the central and southern parts, grasses, low shrubs like willow and birch, and mosses once fed grazing animals such as woolly mammoths, Arctic bison, giant ground sloths, and camels, as well as predators like scimitar cats and lions. Later, moose, elk, and sheep inhabited the shrubby tundra.

How do we know what grew and lived there? Scientists have found remains of plant pollen in sediment samples taken from the ocean floor in the Bering Strait and from the Alaskan tundra. They have even found fossils of beetles. The frozen remains of grazing animals have been studied, and scientists have been able to determine what they ate. Even more amazing, the burned remnants of animal bones are a strong clue that people had enough wood to build fires. Such evidence helps support the theory that humans lived in Beringia until the Ice Age waned and a gradual warming encouraged them to move east, then south. As that same warming caused sea levels to rise, water eventually cut off the trail behind them, keeping them from returning to Siberia. Only a few islands are still visible in the Bering Strait, the last traces of the land bridge.

BLUE BaBe—NOT a TaLL TaLe!

Have you read those stories about Paul Bunyan's blue ox, Babe? Well, maybe they weren't such tall tales after all! In 1979, gold miners in Alaska, using high-pressure water hoses to thaw permafrost and free up gold, uncovered a different kind of treasure: a steppe bison—an Ice Age grazing animal of northern lands. They called their well-preserved specimen Blue Babe, because its skin had turned blue from minerals in the soil where it was found. The bison had frozen quickly and remained almost intact, undisturbed by moving glaciers, for 36,000 years. The carcass was so complete, in fact, that researchers saw claw and tooth marks from the Ice Age lion that had killed it, and smelled its rotting flesh as it thawed.

Blue Babe, on display at the Museum of the North in Fairbanks, Alaska

Where Did Everyone Come From?

People have long wondered about the beginnings of the modern human species we call *Homo sapiens*. Studies of DNA show links between people who lived in eastern Africa around 200,000 years ago and every one of us living on Earth today. But how did those early people come to populate the whole world? Archaeologists have found evidence that they began to move from Africa through Europe and Asia about 55,000 years ago. From northeastern Asia, Beringia provided one path to another continent: North America.

Glaciers like this one once covered much of North America

Scientists have developed theories to explain how this journey might have happened. Northeastern Asia is so remote that much remains to be studied, but a few artifacts have been discovered showing that people lived there about 25,000 years ago. It seems unlikely, though, that they could have survived through the worst of the glacial period, when ice sheets 2 kilometers (1.2 miles) thick—think of six Eiffel Towers stacked one atop the other!—lay over much of the northern hemisphere. After all, modern humans originated in tropical lands and needed time to adapt to harsh northern climates, especially to frigid winters.

However, what if people had already found their way to Beringia, an area too dry to be covered by ice? Some scientists now think this could have been the case. They call parts of that region a *refugium* (a refuge or sanctuary)—land exposed while glaciers held so much water in their icy grip that sea levels dropped about the height of a skyscraper. It's possible that plant and animal species survived there for up to 10,000 years. So early people would have had food and fuel, even in a cold climate. But proof has been hard to find because much of that land now lies under the sea.

DISEASES DIDN'T MAKE THE JOURNEY?

Europeans arriving in North America in the 16th century brought momentous changes, some of them disastrous. Diseases like smallpox had been unknown among aboriginal peoples, so they were defenseless, with no immunity. But if the theory is correct that the aboriginal peoples of North America traveled first through Europe and Asia to cross the Bering Land Bridge, why hadn't these diseases been with them from the beginning?

Researchers think the small groups of people who first entered the continent through Beringia were so isolated by time, distance, and the glacial climate that diseases originating in Europe, usually from domesticated animals, were not present in their population.

American Arrival

If PEOPLE DID ACTUALLY LIVE in Beringia, their descendants appear to have moved into North America beginning around 15,000 years ago. That's when the great ice sheets that still blanketed much of the northern lands began to melt. The change in climate might have prompted people to move on, or perhaps their population had outgrown the food supply. Whatever the reason, while most scientists agree about the time frame, opinions differ widely on what happened next. Some think the gradual melting of the ice may also have opened up an overland passageway on the east side of the Rocky Mountains about 12,500 years ago. If so, early hunter-gatherers could have used

A stamp from around 1991 commemorates the first people to cross into America

it to reach warmer southern areas. Evidence to support this idea—the discovery of carved spear points in Clovis, New Mexico—turned up in 1932. But wait...the "Clovis points" were dated to 13,500 years ago, which suggests human presence 1,000 years or so earlier than anyone would have traveled through that ice-free corridor.

Though we don't know when the migrations happened, we do know that similar stone spear points turned up in many locations across the continent, and even in South America. That means the people who made them spread out, and eventually became the various indigenous peoples that still populate North and South America.

Going South?

WHILE MORE AND MORE CLUES prove the link between early Asian and North American populations, it appears the earliest people to populate what is now Chile may also have ancestral links to Australia and Melanesia, in the western Pacific. The links aren't strong enough to suggest that those people ever sailed directly to South America, and no clues, such as remains of watercraft, have been found. Instead, some of the same group that started their journey in Asia might have moved into both areas—the southern Pacific and through Beringia—up to 2,000 years before the group that settled in North America. The scientific world is excited by the possibility that people reached South America by moving down the coast from Beringia, possibly using small boats over a route believed to be ice free during part of the Ice Age. Any traces of early humans there are now buried under the sea, but was that the route they used to reach the southern continent?

Unraveling the Mysteries

Sorting out these ideas is a bit like trying to put together a jigsaw puzzle with many pieces missing—and no picture on the lid of the box. As new discoveries are made and genetic details are analyzed, fresh theories are proposed. That's how science works: research may lead to answers, but it always stirs up more questions, too. Of course, not everyone agrees with these theories. The spiritual traditions of aboriginal peoples live in their creation stories, and through these spoken tales, they share their beliefs about their presence in North America. It was only after the first Europeans landed on this continent in the 16th century that any written records of human activities were kept.

In the Bering Land Bridge National Preserve, archaeologists continue to find evidence that humans used this land route so long ago. And they've found examples of nearly identical plants and animals that once lived on both sides of the Bering Strait. So the bridge did exist.

While we don't know for sure where the first North Americans came from, when they arrived, or exactly how they came to live here, it is clear that early people faced enormous challenges to survive and adapt. Over thousands of years, they conquered obstacles to thrive in all sorts of environments across the continent, from deserts to forests to plains.

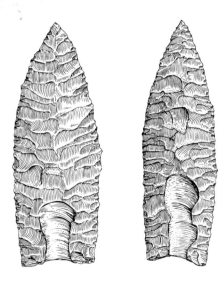

MORE PIECES OF THE PUZZLE

Tools, bones, and other evidence of humans help archaeologists piece together when and how people migrated to the Americas. Here are some of the most important discoveries.

KENNEWICK MAN, found in 1996 alongside the Columbia River in Washington State and studied using genome sequencing (uncoding a long string of genetic information), has been found to be around 9,000 years old and of Native American ancestry.

ANZICK BOY, found in Montana in 1968, was a young child buried beneath many Clovis points. Genome sequencing links these 12,600-year-old remains to early Asians, but also shows the boy was a direct ancestor of aboriginal people in Central and South America.

PAISLEY FIVE MILE POINT CAVES in southern Oregon is the site of the oldest human DNA found so far in America. Samples of feces (poop!) show humans lived there 14,300 years ago.

BUTTERMILK CREEK, TEXAS, has turned up stone tools dating from 15,500 years ago that were small and light enough for people on the move to carry easily.

ROMAN ROADS

Designed for Conquest

NAME

Some of the major Roman roads include
Fosse Way, Ermine Street, and Watling Street.

AGE

Roman conquerors built roads to link the far-flung centers of their empire, particularly in Britain, between 43 and 410 CE. But carbon dating shows that earlier civilizations, the Celts and Druids, built parts of Britain's road system between the fourth and first centuries BCE. Romans likely placed some of their roads on top of those earlier tracks.

CLAIM TO FAME

Roman roads are famous for their solid and enduring construction. Some stretches of road more than 1,600 years old can still be seen; others became the foundation for modern highways. Linking major population centers in Britain, the roads formed an efficient transport and communication system for armies, travelers, and tradespeople and became critical to the development of the mighty Roman Empire.

NORTH ATLANTIC OCEAN

Dere

York

NORTH SEA

IRELAND

BRITAIN

Chester

Lincoln

Watling

Ermine

Fosse Way

Akeman

London

Portway

WHO USES THEM NOW?

If you follow Britain's main highways, you'll quite likely be driving over some buried Roman roads. In London, Oxford Street and Bayswater Road were built on the old roads.

DESCRIPTION

The Roman network of roads crisscrossed Britain, from the south coast to Hadrian's Wall in the north (almost to today's Scottish border), and from the east coast to the western frontier with Wales. It totaled between 13,000 and 16,000 kilometers (8,000 to 10,000 miles).

Fosse Way
64 CE

The sound of horses' hooves on the cobbled road draws Jon and his mother to the doorway of their small thatched-roof home. A Roman cavalry soldier comes into view, leading a troop of foot soldiers through the village to a military post nearby. Jon hopes they won't march straight through without stopping to buy food and drink. Villagers like his mother operate stalls in front of their homes along the busy road that runs to the city of Lincoln. These soldiers might offer metal coins for cobs of bread she's baked from wheat grown in fields outside the village, or for wine that she gets from a traveling Roman merchant. If they do, Jon's mother will give him some money to buy carrots and cabbage from one of the farm carts pulled by oxen that pass by on the road. The vegetables will go into the stew she'll cook over the fire for their meal that day.

The cavalry soldier stops, and orders the rest of the troop to halt behind him. The soldiers lay down their shields and spears before a few of them approach Jon's mother's stall. While walking down the muddy laneway from the paved road, one soldier drops something he's pulled from a small pouch. He looks upset, stooping down to dig around in the mud. The other soldiers jostle him and laugh as they trample the ground where he's searching.

Jon doesn't understand the language they're speaking, but he knows whatever the soldier lost must be important. The order is given to resume their march, and the unhappy soldier turns away without buying anything. It must have been a coin, Jon thinks. He'll wait until the troop moves off and then try to find the money himself. If he's successful, maybe tonight's supper will have a bit of pork or rabbit meat in it, too.

The Story of Roman Roads in Britain

F ROM ITS BEGINNINGS in about 31 BCE when the first emperor, Augustus Caesar, came to power, the warlike Roman Empire expanded to include most of the countries surrounding the Mediterranean Sea. Once these lands were conquered by military might, Rome controlled them by building stable economies, and using the resources from farmland, forests, and mines to fuel the business of the vast empire. The key to holding onto and managing territory was well-built roads: Romans eventually built about 88,500 kilometers (55,000 miles) of roads throughout their empire. You'd have to cross the United States about 26 times to travel that far!

Roman roads across the empire were built to last for centuries

Naturally, when the Roman Empire overpowered Britain, it needed an effective transportation network to link main population centers. Once roads were built, settlements and markets emerged at crossroads and river crossings, growing into small towns. So the roads helped both the economy and society to grow. And the Romans did such a good job of road-building that many parts have withstood the wear and tear of centuries. It is remarkable that even with a huge realm to maintain, they took such great care and trouble building roads in Britain, one of the most remote—and final—parts of their empire to be conquered.

The Romans Are Coming!

IT WAS THE FOURTH EMPEROR, Claudius, who invaded Britain, in 43 CE. He chose Britain more to ensure his reputation as a military leader than for the value of its trade or industry. To the emperor, the country was an easy target because the diverse groups that lived there were unlikely to resist occupation. A quick victory would boost his image with all Romans.

It all went well for Claudius in Britain's south and east, where he overran the local people and their capital city, now called Colchester. With his new status secured, he proudly returned to Rome to rule until 54 CE. Roman armies continued to take over more of Britain. When some of the local people refused to give in, Roman soldiers laid siege. In the Midlands, for example, the Welsh put up a fight that dragged on for almost 20 years.

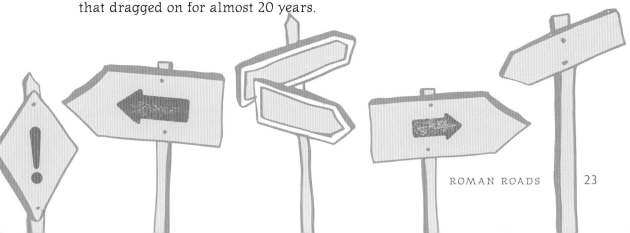

Hadrian's Wall

Although rebellion flared up again in eastern Britain, by 84 CE the Romans had rolled over all resistance and moved north almost as far as the present-day border with Scotland. Roughly 40 years later, from 120 to 130 CE, Emperor Hadrian built a stone wall stretching 117 kilometers (73 miles) across the narrowest part of Britain to mark the northern limit of Roman occupation. Beyond that wall were the "barbarians" of Scotland. Despite the Romans' repeated attempts to conquer Scotland as well, the fierce Scottish tribes held them off.

The Romans would remain in Britain for another 350 years, until Rome itself was attacked by the armies of the Visigoths, from eastern Europe. When that happened, Roman troops were hastily withdrawn and sent home to defend the empire.

Why Build Roads?

THE ROMAN INVASION involved thousands of troops, along with their horses and carts loaded with weapons, armor, and other equipment. Good roads were essential to move such a fighting force over long distances, through all kinds of terrain and in all weather. The Romans wanted fast access to send reinforcements to battle sites, and reliable routes to resupply soldiers with food and equipment. Roads were kept in top condition because they allowed swift communication between forts, which helped the invaders maintain control of conquered territory and exchange news with the rest of the empire. Later, these roads linked the towns that grew around the forts, and were used by tradesmen and farmers taking their goods to market. Manufactured goods made of pottery, metal, and glass imported from Europe became easily available to those living in outlying areas.

Roman "Camps"

On a map of Britain, you'll see many towns with names that end in suffixes like -chester (Winchester), -caster (Doncaster) or -cester (Gloucester). These cities would have started out as military towns, or "camps," housing soldiers and all their equipment when they were not marching or fighting. The Latin word for "camp" is castrum, which is the source for these names that have remained. In much the same way, towns in Wales like Caerleon and Caerwent take their names from the Welsh term caer, meaning "fortified city."

Groma

Roman surveyors used a simple direction-finding tool called a *groma*. Two pieces of wood of equal length were crossed at the center. Then a plumb line (a weighted string to show a true vertical line) was hung from each of the four tips. This cross was mounted on the end of a horizontal arm set to rotate on a pole stuck in the ground. A fifth plumb line hung from the center of the crossed pieces. An assistant, standing on a high point of ground, could then line up the fifth plumb line with one of the other four on the *groma* to determine a straight path and mark it with a stake. That line would become the path of the road. Today, surveyors use a far more sophisticated instrument called a theodolite.

Skilled by Experience

THE ROMANS KNEW ROAD-BUILDING. Before they brought their skills to Britain, they had built the first road networks all over Europe. It was part of a soldier's duty to serve as surveyor, engineer, or construction crew. Slaves from the local area were also put to work.

Surveyors carefully explored the terrain to find the straightest possible route between locations, and to avoid difficult obstacles like swamps, forests, and hills. They used a tool called a *groma*, a simple instrument made of wood and string, to find the best path. Trees were cleared if necessary. Since no heavy equipment existed at that time, all the work was done with hand tools.

Roads were typically constructed using whatever type of stony material was handy. Builders would begin by creating a ridge called an agger (an embankment). In some cases, the agger sat at a height close to the eye level of an average-sized elephant and was wide enough for two horse-drawn, two-wheeled carts to pass each other. The height prevented flooding in low-lying areas, and gave soldiers a good view of the surrounding countryside. This kept them safe from attacks by hostile locals who had not yet surrendered to the invaders.

The material that was dug to form the ridge left open ditches on either side for drainage. The ridges were often topped with layers of sand, gravel, or flint (a hard stone) pounded to a firm base. Many roads in towns were paved (called *metalled* in Britain) with large, flat stones found locally, laid close together to form a long-lasting surface.

A Roman milestone

When the road met a river, it might simply cross it at a shallow, paved ford. Wooden bridges were built over wider rivers. During Roman times, it was usually only the bridges that needed repairs. The roads were built to stand up under heavy military traffic, so it's no wonder some of them lasted for centuries.

Milestones—tall, rounded stones—guided travelers at regular intervals, showing information about the distance to a destination. Some had the name of the ruling emperor engraved or painted on them, details that have helped archaeologists determine the date of a road's construction. About every 20 kilometers (12 miles), rest stations and supply posts called *mutationes* allowed travelers to change horses. Then, after traveling twice that distance again, they could eat, sleep, and bathe, as well as stable their horses, in larger inns called *mansios*.

A Few Major Roads

ONE OF THE EARLIEST—and straightest—roads built by the Romans
was called the **Fosse Way**. The name comes from the Latin *fossa*, meaning
"ditch," perhaps because the invading Romans marked and defended the
newly taken western edge of their empire with trenches. This military
route, built in the middle of the first century CE, traced a diagonal line
across the country as a direct path to move troops and transport goods
to the north. The journey was at least a nine-day march for foot soldiers,
and took about a month in a much slower cart or wagon. Today, you can
make the same trip in a few hours on modern highways built nearby.

From Exeter in the southwest, Fosse Way ran through the major
military posts (now cities) of Bath, Cirencester, and Leicester, and ended at
Lincoln. Exeter was captured from the Celts and became a Roman fortress
city in 46 CE. Being close to the sea, it was used as a port for Roman
armies to enter Britain. At Bath, the Romans established a hot-water spa,

The Roman-built spa in Bath

which they named *Aquae Sulis.* Farther northeast, Cirencester was a busy market center, known for wool. Just north of the intersection with another main Roman road, **Watling Street,** Fosse Way continued through the military settlement of Leicester, and on to the fortress of Lincoln, built in 60 CE.

Another major road was **Ermine Street**, built between 45 and 75 CE, with much of it still in existence today. Ermine Street began in the great city of London and ran north through Lincoln all the way to York. Also called the Great North Road, this direct connection was vital for supplying armies in the north, and bringing goods from farmlands on the eastern side of the country. With many settlements along the way, it was well situated for distributing trade goods, too. **Dere Street**, built around 80 CE, ran on from York all the way up to Hadrian's Wall.

Watling Street (the name is from Old English—history doesn't tell us what the Romans called it), a third main road, ran east to west instead of north to south. Built in 48 CE, it began at Dover on the English Channel—the closest seaport for Romans entering Britain from continental Europe. From London, it went all the way to Wales.

A Battle along the Road

ALTHOUGH THE ROADS made getting around Britain easier for everyone, the conquering Romans did not find a welcome reception everywhere they went. Watling Street was the site of a fierce battle in 60 CE between Roman forces and a Celtic tribe from the east led by their queen, Boudica.

The queen was looking for revenge against the Roman emperor, Nero. Boudica's husband had been

Boudica, depicted in a 19th-century illustration

a puppet ruler—he'd had no real power and could only do what Rome ordered—but when he died, he left Boudica and his daughters half of his land. Emperor Nero took all of the property, though, and used many of the people living there as slaves. When Boudica objected she was flogged, a serious and painful public humiliation.

While the Roman army was busy putting down a revolt in the west, Boudica saw her opportunity. Well trained as a fighter, she led over 100,000 followers in an attack against the fortress of Colchester, killing every Roman there. London was the next target of her wrath— it was burned and many people were massacred. Finally, she wiped out the fortress of St. Albans. Somewhere near High Cross, Boudica's forces had to pass through a valley toward 10,000 Roman soldiers, who used the advantage of their hilltop position to defeat her. It is not certain how Boudica died, but the Romans brutally executed her people and took over their lands, and the rebellion was over.

WALLED CITIES

Roman invaders used barricades of earth around their fortresses to protect their soldiers from hostile local people. Later, many of these barriers were rebuilt using stone, and the stone walls could be long enough to encircle an entire city. After the Romans left Britain, their original walls were sometimes built higher and stronger by the next invaders.

The cities of Chester and York have preserved their walls as heritage sites. Chester's walls were first built of earth between 70 and 80 CE, and later included arched gates and towers of stone. The city was worth defending: it sat near the border with northern Wales, and was a key port on the River Dee. The Romans built a wall around York in 71 CE. Its four gates determined the pattern of the city's main streets that still survives today.

The walls of York

Gone, but Not Forgotten

During the early fifth century, bands of people called Angles (from Scandinavia), Saxons (from Germany), and Picts (from Scotland) began to attack Britain. At the same time, Roman forces were withdrawn to fight off the Visigoth invaders at home. The Romans never returned to Britain, but the legacy they left was their network of roads, an amazing foundation for today's modern highways.

An old Roman road near Manchester, England

An old Roman fort can be seen using LIDAR

NO LONGER VISIBLE....

Sections of ancient Roman roads can easily be seen throughout Britain's countryside, and archaeologists work to preserve this proof of Roman presence centuries ago. But many more roads lie hidden beneath the ground, buried by the effects of 1,600 years of weather and human changes to the land.

Recently, the United Kingdom's Environment Agency has used laser technology—LIDAR (light detection and ranging)— to survey the land from aircraft in order to find low-lying areas that might be in danger of flooding. It has turned up exciting surprises. Roman roads were built on rocky ridges raised above the original ground level. The laser imaging shows them lying just below today's soil surface. Even a short portion found by this "eye in the sky" can point archaeologists to long stretches of previously invisible roads.

3

CAMINO DE SANTIAGO

Pathways to Faith

NAME

Camino is Spanish for "path" or "road," and Santiago de Compostela is the name of a cathedral at its end. *Sant Iago* is Spanish for "Saint James." *Compostela* is thought to come from either the Latin *campus stellae*, meaning "field of stars," or *compositum*, meaning "cemetery." Also known as The Way of Saint James, or just The Way.

AGE

Pilgrims began visiting Santiago de Compostela in the early 800s. The first written record of the pilgrimage dates back to 950 CE.

DESCRIPTION

The Camino de Santiago is a network of ancient routes that lead to the cathedral of Santiago de Compostela in Galicia, a province of northwestern Spain. Pilgrims follow well-marked tracks along modern paved roads as well as rough trails linking communities. At least a dozen named trails begin at different starting points in Spain, France, and Portugal.

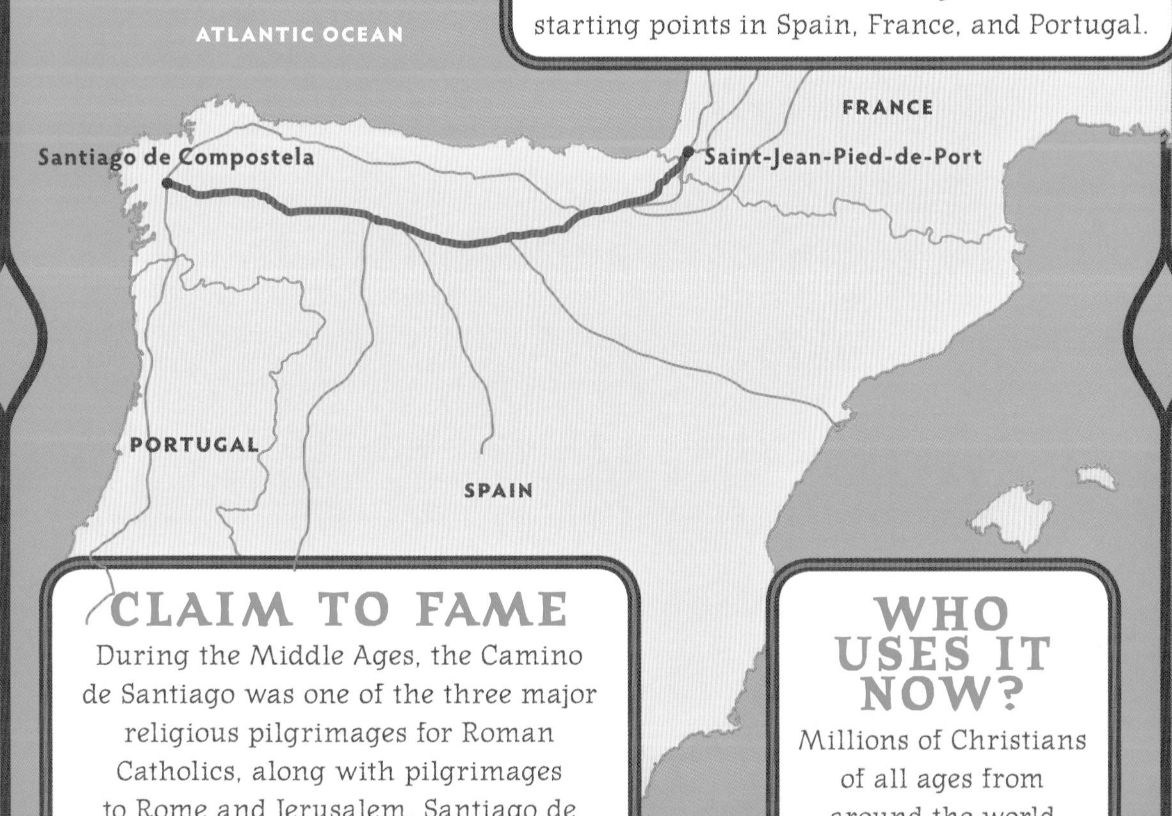

ATLANTIC OCEAN

FRANCE

Santiago de Compostela

Saint-Jean-Pied-de-Port

PORTUGAL

SPAIN

CLAIM TO FAME

During the Middle Ages, the Camino de Santiago was one of the three major religious pilgrimages for Roman Catholics, along with pilgrimages to Rome and Jerusalem. Santiago de Compostela was named a UNESCO World Heritage Site in 1985, and the route was included in the Council of Europe Cultural Routes in 1987.

WHO USES IT NOW?

Millions of Christians of all ages from around the world walk the Camino each year. Seekers of spiritual or cultural wisdom, those on a personal mission, tourists, and athletes all set out on the route.

A village in northern Spain
1980s

Afternoons are Mateo's favorite time of day during summer holidays. After spending the early morning hours helping his parents and older sister clean the rooms in their albergue, he can watch for the next group of peregrinos to arrive. His family's hostel is one of many along the route of the Camino de Santiago, and it's popular because his parents provide a family dinner. Other hostels offer breakfast instead, but Mateo likes being able to spend time with the pilgrims at the end of their day. Even if he can't always understand the different languages they speak, it's fun to make friends during their short stays.

Most of the pilgrims are up by 5:00 or 6:00 a.m., ready to hit the road on the next leg of their trek to Santiago de Compostela. Then, the dorm rooms must be swept and dusted, the showers and toilets cleaned, and the laundry room made ready for the next group to wash their clothes. While it's quiet by mid-morning in Mateo's albergue, the day soon gets busy again. Tired, dusty hikers begin to show up in the early afternoon. Mateo helps check in the new arrivals, shows them a bunk, and tells them where they can buy food for the next day. Most of the pilgrims like to shower and do laundry before wandering around the town. But they all gather at the big dining table in the evening for the authentic Spanish food that Mateo's parents cook. The meat, vegetable, and rice stew called paella is one of Mateo's favorites, along with churros (doughnuts) dusted with cinnamon for dessert. Sometimes they'll spend the evening singing folk songs or sharing stories of each day's travels until everyone turns in at 10:00 p.m. One day, Mateo hopes to hike trails in other countries just as these pilgrims are doing.

A trail marker on the Camino de Santiago

The Story of Camino de Santiago

IF YOU'VE EVER TAKEN A HIKE in the countryside carrying a backpack with a little food and extra clothing, you've traveled much as pilgrims of all ages have done for hundreds of years. More than just a hike, though, a religious pilgrimage usually follows a route to a specific place made famous by the story of a holy person.

Spain's Camino de Santiago is a network of ancient pilgrim routes. They may begin at various points across the country, or at a person's home, but the final destination is the same: the medieval city of Santiago de Compostela in northwest Spain. Inside that city's grand ninth-century cathedral, a statue of Saint James adorns the high altar. Roman Catholics believe his remains are buried in a silver casket that rests in the chapel beneath.

A Turbulent History

THE COUNTRY WE CALL SPAIN today has seen a number of ruling empires come and go. In its early days, around 600 BCE, settlers who may have come from North Africa populated its eastern and southern coasts. Later, Celts came from Central Europe, and Greeks and Carthaginians from the eastern Mediterranean.

Around 200 BCE, as the Roman Empire expanded, its rulers took over the territory, known by the Greek name *Iberia*, and renamed it *Hispania*, or Spain. Evidence of their 500-year presence can be seen in what's left of Roman-style roads, bridges, and aqueducts, and heard in the Spanish language, based on the Latin spoken by Romans. Visigoths controlled the territory in the sixth century, after the Romans left, and they in turn were pushed out in the eighth century by the Moors, who swept in from North Africa to occupy Spain until the end of the 15th century.

WHAT IS A PILGRIMAGE?

Usually, "pilgrimage" describes a journey to a particular place of special significance. If it is a religious place—a church or shrine—those who visit feel their prayers, offered so close to a spiritual presence, will bring comfort for personal troubles, or wisdom to improve their lives. Each year for centuries, millions of people have visited Jerusalem in Israel, Mecca in Saudi Arabia, and the Golden Temple in India—all sacred places in their different religions. Some pilgrims set off not to follow a specific path or reach a certain destination, but simply to wander and spread the word of their faith.

Not all pilgrimages are made for religious reasons. A modern journey might lead to a historic site such as the First and Second World War cemeteries in Europe, or an artist's birthplace, such as rock-and-roll icon Elvis Presley's Graceland home in Tennessee.

The Legend of Saint James

LEGENDS SAY THAT JAMES, one of the 12 apostles of Jesus, came to Spain to spread the Christian message following Jesus's crucifixion. When he returned to Jerusalem, as described in the Bible, he was beheaded by King Herod Agrippa I in 42 CE. Friends then took his body by boat to Spain and hid it in a field near the northwest coast. In the Middle Ages the remains were discovered, so it is told, by a shepherd led there by a bright star (perhaps the origin of the name *compostela*). After identification by a local bishop, the relics were taken for reburial.

King Alfonso II, ruler of the Visigoths, who held the territory at that time, declared James the patron saint of Spain and built a small cathedral in his honor. Later, King Alfonso III rebuilt it, and pilgrims began to trek to Santiago de Compostela to express their faith. The cathedral was eventually destroyed by the Muslim Moors, who were fighting the Visigoths for control of the region. Out of respect for the tomb of Saint James, however, they left it undamaged. The church that stands today was rebuilt in the 11th century.

Word soon spread of miracles linked to Saint James: it was told that he appeared as a knight on a white horse to encourage Christian soldiers in battles against the Moors. Early Christians also believed that illnesses could be cured through prayer to such a powerful saint. The pilgrimage attracted more and more people—up to half a million during the 11th and 12th centuries. It became even more important to Christians than older pilgrim routes to Rome and Jerusalem. (Jerusalem in particular had become a difficult place for Christians to reach after the Crusades in the Middle Ages failed to take the Holy Land from Muslim control.)

Monasteries and churches popped up along the route, while bridges and hostels were built to provide pilgrims with help along the way. Hospitals were established to care for the many people who, even though they were ill, walked the route in hopes of a cure. And the money that flowed into the region supported a long military campaign called the *Reconquista*, which saw Christians trying to take back territory in Spain from the Moors. Wars in Europe over the next few centuries slowed the flow of pilgrims, but today over 2.5 million people—religious pilgrims, tourists, and hikers alike—walk the Camino and visit the sacred site of Santiago de Compostela each year.

Pilgrims visit the cathedral

Mecca and the Golden Temple

The teachings of Islam include five basic practices. The fifth of these concerns the "House of God," built in Mecca, Saudi Arabia, by the prophet Abraham. During daily prayers, Muslims around the world face this holy site. A pilgrimage called *hajj*, which the Quran (the holy book of Islam) urges Muslims to undertake at least once in their lives, is meant to renew believers' faith by bringing them together to worship as equals.

For followers of another ancient religion, Sikhism, a holy shrine in Amritsar, India, is their central religious place. Built in the middle of a small lake, the Golden Temple symbolizes the Sikh beliefs in brotherhood and equality. Its four entrances facing different directions welcome anyone to meditate there, just as the founder of the religion, Guru Nanak, once did.

The Golden Temple

Hiking the Trail

ONE OF THE most famous and popular tracks on this network of roads is called the *Camino Francés*, or French Way. This route begins in the foothills of the Pyrenees mountains that divide Spain and France. On its way west, the route passes through rural areas, small villages, and historic cities. The trails include busy, paved public roads or tracks beside them, narrow country lanes, and simple, quiet dirt or stone footpaths. Parts of some routes follow the original straight Roman roads. The way might be hilly, flat, or wooded. It may wind through open farm fields amid flocks of sheep, or follow a river.

Saint-Jean-Pied-de-Port, the starting point of the Camino Francés

Today, most pilgrims follow this route on foot, while some ride bicycles or horses. A typical hiker might make the entire journey in about a month. They travel the trail in all weather and in all seasons for days, weeks, or months, stopping overnight at the numerous hostels and small inns. Markers along the way guide walkers in the right direction. Water fonts are available to refill drinking bottles. Pilgrims choose their own pace, depending on the time they have, their level of fitness, and their personal goal for the journey. Some are looking for spiritual comfort. Some want to enjoy the history and culture of Spain.

THE SCALLOP SHELL SYMBOL

Along the route to Santiago de Compostela, signposts and buildings are decorated with a scallop shell. Pilgrims carry one, or wear the shell like a badge on their clothes. How did it come to be the symbol of Saint James? Stories tell of a horse and rider, with white scallop shells clinging to his clothes, saved from drowning in the sea at the spot where the apostle's body was brought to the Spanish coast. It's also said that James's body, lost in a storm, was washed ashore covered with the shells. The stories are kept alive by this easily recognized emblem of the pilgrimage.

Some see the trek mainly as challenging physical exercise. Others want to experience a peaceful time to resolve personal problems; many make a conscious decision to leave their cellphones at home. Watches are often left behind, too, letting hikers learn to judge time of day by the position of the sun, length of shadows, their hunger, or their tired feet.

Each pilgrim carries a *credential* (passport) which is stamped with official seals at hostels, churches, monasteries, or town halls to prove they have actually covered the route. A pilgrim must walk at least 100 kilometers (62 miles) to earn a certificate of completion upon reaching Santiago de Compostela. There, pilgrims light candles and gather each day at noon to hear mass in different languages and tour the historic building. Some people choose to continue their trek to Finisterre (meaning "end of the Earth"). The legend of Saint James arose in this coastal village, where it is said his bones were first discovered.

It is remarkable that today this symbolic route—the Camino de Santiago—still has the power to draw so many who want to walk in the steps of pilgrims before them, who want to test themselves against a physical challenge, or who seek to understand and perhaps renew their faith.

THE APPALACHIAN TRAIL

This trail through the forested lands of America's Appalachian Mountains was built only as a footpath—the longest in the world. Bikes and horses are not allowed, except on a few short sections. Most hikers begin in Georgia and head north through 14 states, finishing in Maine—a trip that may take five to seven months. Anyone who manages to complete the entire length in a single trip is called a "thru-hiker." But many more return year after year to take on parts of the trail. Each year, thousands of people of all ages hike and camp along this highly popular route. Like pilgrims on the Camino de Santiago, they come for various reasons: a personal search for peace, an extreme exercise challenge, or simply to enjoy the outdoors.

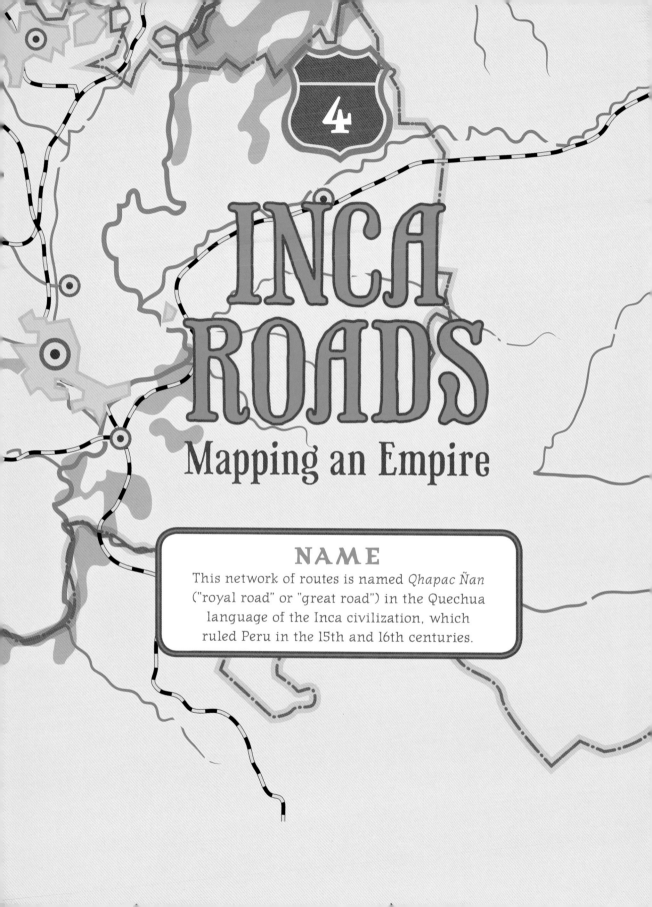

4

INCA ROADS

Mapping an Empire

NAME

This network of routes is named *Qhapac Ñan*
("royal road" or "great road") in the Quechua
language of the Inca civilization, which
ruled Peru in the 15th and 16th centuries.

AGE

Developed by the Inca Empire in the centuries before Spanish conquest in 1532, the roads were built on pre-Inca trails dating back 2,500 years.

DESCRIPTION

This road system in South America linked Colombia, Ecuador, Bolivia, Peru, Chile, and Argentina. From Cuzco, capital of the Inca Empire (in modern-day Peru), roads fanned out in four directions to reach all parts of the empire. A main north–south road ran through the Andes highlands. A similar coastal route was connected to it by a web of secondary roads.

COLOMBIA

Quito

ECUADOR

Tumbes

PERU

BRAZIL

Lima

Cuzco

BOLIVIA

La Paz

PACIFIC OCEAN

CHILE

ARGENTINA

Santiago

Mendoza

CLAIM TO FAME

The Inca road system is recognized as an amazing example of 16th-century engineering skill. In 2014, the Qhapac Ñan became a UNESCO World Heritage Site, to be restored and preserved from future loss.

WHO USES THEM NOW?

Villagers still use the original roads to travel and trade with neighboring communities. The route is also popular with hikers and tourists who visit ancient sites such as Machu Picchu. But modern visitors must be guided in small groups, and follow new regulations designed to prevent littering and erosion.

On the Road to Cuzco
1520

Wayra breathes deeply as his strong leg muscles power him over the rocky trail. Already several kilometers from the fishing port of Puerto Inca, he sees his path climbing steeply up the terraced hillside. He knows he has to keep running at top speed for the 15 minutes or so it will take him to reach the tampu, a station where he will hand over his package to a fresh runner. Wayra and the other chasquis have been trained since they were small boys to run fast—as fast as the wind he is named for—and to develop their lungs in the thin Andean mountain air. It is a hard task, but one he is happy to know he will do all his life.

As his sandals steadily slap the ground, Wayra is glad his burdens are light. The loose tunic he wears and blanket he carries for nighttime are both made from soft, warm llama wool. He grips the knotted string quipu that helps him remember information to deliver, and the pututu made from a conch shell to trumpet his arrival at the next station. A woven qipi sack hangs from his shoulder. Wrapped tightly inside is the precious cargo of a fresh tuna. That fish is the reason for his haste along the trail. It has to reach the palace in Cuzco in just one day, to be served to the emperor. Wayra knows it will be so, even though he will not carry it the whole way himself. His bundle will be passed along the road from one chasqui to the next, always moving toward its destination. Wayra will also share the messages he's been entrusted with memorizing, some of the details encoded in the knots of the quipu so he won't forget anything. Then he can rest until another chasqui comes running down the trail, and Wayra will take over the next leg of a new relay.

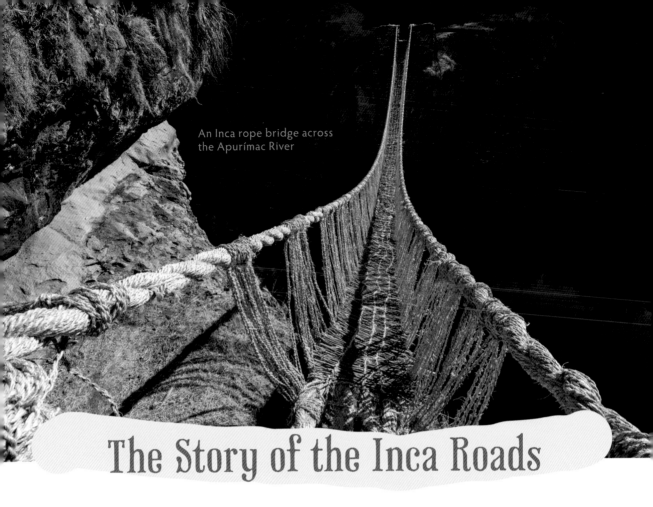

An Inca rope bridge across the Apurímac River

The Story of the Inca Roads

THE INCA EMPIRE ROSE in the 1400s from a small civilization of warrior kings and peasants living in the Cuzco Valley near Lake Titicaca. After conquering neighboring kingdoms, the ambitious Inca continued to swallow up land and people. Within about 50 years, they had created a powerful empire along the Andes and the Pacific coast. At the height of its power, the empire took in six countries and up to 10 million people and was the richest, most advanced society in South America.

So how did a small army of invaders from Spain, a nation on the other side of the world, overcome the Inca Empire in only a few years? Ironically, one of the Inca's most impressive accomplishments—the extensive road system that tied the empire together—was key to its downfall. It allowed the Spanish conquerors who arrived in the 1500s to penetrate its heart, eventually crush its defenses, and virtually wipe out a people who had ruled for barely 100 years.

The Reasons for Roads

PARTS OF THE INCA ROAD SYSTEM were developed from trails known as early as 1000 BCE. It's unlikely the empire would have become so strong or wealthy without a well-built road system. How else would Inca rulers have expanded over such challenging terrain and overcome such enormous geographical obstacles? Their network of roads allowed them not only to trade with other societies, but also to conquer new territory over vast distances. Afterward, they were able to more easily defend and control their empire through constant communication and trade. Whenever a new Inca ruler came to power, he would visit the outlying areas of the empire to reinforce relationships and renew agreements with the people under his authority. That kind of management succeeded, in part, because goods and services flowed easily along the roads, satisfying people's needs and holding the empire together.

Taking Cues from Nature

HISTORIANS CONTINUE TO MARVEL at the impressive accomplishments of Inca engineers. The skills they developed for building with nothing more than basic wood, stone, and bronze tools did not show up anywhere else in the world for centuries. Roads through the Andes, the world's longest mountain range, were usually kept below an elevation of 5,000 meters (16,400 feet) since high mountain climates pose difficult conditions. Even so, Inca engineers faced the challenges of a wide variety of landscapes: the grasslands of the lowland river valleys, coastal deserts, forested slopes, narrow rocky ledges through mountain passes, and tangled rainforest undergrowth.

A rock stairway

Whatever these builders created—structures as well as roads—they preserved a sense of harmony with the natural world. To do so, they used all the materials available to them, including both living and non-living matter. Rocks were a basic construction material. So were natural fibers such as grass. The only beast of burden they knew was the llama, so it became their working partner in every possible way.

Roads ranged from the width of a sidewalk to that of three sidewalks placed side by side. Archaeologists have discovered that, where possible, the roads followed straight lines, like the rock-bordered causeways laid out across flat grasslands. Even where the ground was not flat, the track was kept to an even grade—that means a road that curved around a hillside did not climb higher and dip lower, but stayed at the same level. Where hills were very steep, sections of rock stairways ran up, or roads ran back and forth across the hills in switchback style. Over long distances, travel on such roads was less tiring for both humans and pack animals. If you've ever hiked in the mountains, you'll know how much more energy it takes to go straight uphill, and how hard it is to keep your footing when you're coming straight down!

The Andes region is subject to heavy seasonal rains and snow-melt runoff. How did the Inca stop water from ruining their roads? If road surfaces were covered with uneven paving stones, they discovered, it broke up torrents of water, slowing it and giving it time to seep away harmlessly. A raised row of stones laid across a sloping road also interrupted water flow and pushed it sideways, and culverts—structures that ran across either on top of or under the road—funneled the water into drainage ditches. Stone walls bordering the road allowed runoff to drain through small gaps instead of eroding the road edges. These walls also protected crops planted on either side, which kept travelers on the path.

We know many of these facts because the road system was so well built it withstood centuries of weathering, erosion, and even the many earthquakes common to this region (part of what's known as the Ring of Fire, around the Pacific Ocean). Many sections of Inca roads remain intact, and in fact are still regularly used by local inhabitants.

Llamas

The two-toed, padded feet of llamas made them the perfect pack animals for the Inca Road—their feet don't damage the road surfaces, and llama-trekking is still one of the best ways to travel in fragile environments. Able to carry up to 34 kilograms (75 pounds), or the weight of two or three concrete blocks, these long-necked camel relatives served the Inca in other ways, too. Their hides provided leather for sandals, their wool made warm clothing, and their meat could be eaten. Even their dung was useful; scientists think it was dried for fertilizer that helped maize (corn) grow on fields in high elevations.

Llamas at
Machu Picchu

Tunnels and Bridges

How do you build a tunnel through solid rock without explosives or heavy equipment? The Inca found the smartest answer right under their noses. They understood that when the water in rocks freezes, it expands and causes the rocks to crack. Repeated cracking broke up and loosened the rocks, which could then be removed to create tunnels.

When it came time to cross one of the many swift-flowing rivers, or to span a deep gorge from one sheer rock face to another, something else was needed. A bridge was the answer, of course. Without steel or concrete, the Inca could not build the kind of bridges we see on highways today. Yet Inca engineers created as many as 200 suspension bridges that lasted hundreds of years. One of the longest was over the Apurímac River—as long as three school buses parked end to end. How did they do it?

THE BRIDGE IS MOVING!

Have you ever walked on a suspension bridge? Did you grab the railings when it started to sway and then sagged in the middle? Inca bridges acted the same way: you walked downhill until you reached the lowest point, then had to climb the slope on the second half of the bridge. The Inca knew their bridges were safe, but Spanish soldiers were so afraid of the seemingly flimsy, swinging structures that they crossed them on hands and knees.

The Inca hadn't invented the wheel, so llamas, not carts, had to carry all the building materials they needed. They used abundant matter close at hand—dried grass and other plant fibers—to create rope. Grasses called *ichu* were first twisted to form a narrow cord. Several cords were wound together, then laid out in bundles to be braided. The finished rope might be as thick as your upper body, and incredibly strong.

Workers swam or rafted across the river, or climbed the sides of the canyon to take a narrow rope across the span, then used it to pull four thicker ones across, where they were anchored with towers of rock. These four ropes formed the floor of the bridge. Two more became handrails, held above the floor and joined to it with woven vertical cords, making a walled passageway. More plant fibers were laid over the floor to give firmer footing to walkers and llamas, the only traffic crossing the bridges. When a bridge needed repair, or if the Inca chose to cut or burn one down to deter unwanted raiders, the rebuilding materials were always nearby.

Inca Roads and Roman Roads

Although their civilizations were separated by about 1,000 years and developed half a world apart, the Romans and Incas both built amazing road networks, some of which still exist today. And their work had a lot in common. Both used local materials to construct mostly straight roads that radiated out from a central city. Both paved important roads with large, flat rocks and devised a drainage system to prevent erosion. The Romans built rest stops called *mutationes* and *mansios* along their roads, while the Inca used *tampu* as shelters. Roads in both empires made communication and control by military forces easier, and made it possible to conduct trade over long distances. One major difference stands out, though: horses and carts transported Romans, but the Inca roads saw only foot traffic, or llamas used as pack animals.

Without such well-built roads, neither culture would have been able to take over and control such vast areas. But, ironically, in both cases, the extensive road network allowed new invaders to move in and bring these empires to an end.

A paved Inca road in the Andes Mountains

Who Used the Roads?

OFFICIAL REPRESENTATIVES of the Inca ruler used the road system for state business. They gathered information to report on food production, record population numbers, and keep track of the tributes (payments such as potatoes, alpaca wool, wood or pottery crafts, and gold or silver) that communities were expected to send to the government. The emperor himself and his armies traveled widely to attend ceremonies, maintain order, and conquer new territory.

The roads were also critically important to traders, who carried goods in llama caravans. Everything needed for a thriving economy found its way along the road system: food grown on grasslands and terraced slopes, fish caught at the coast, woven fabrics, weapons, and gold. Ordinary people needed permission or paid tolls to travel on the roads.

HUINCHIRI FESTIVAL

To keep the ancient art of building grass bridges alive and pass it along to future generations, local inhabitants of four villages in a valley near Huinchiri, Peru, hold a special ceremony each June. They rebuild a suspension bridge called *kewsha chaca* in the traditional way, using braided grass. It takes three days to complete, the operation closely watched by the *chacacamayoc*, or bridge keeper. Then the previous year's bridge is cut down and the river carries it away. The people can rightly claim that this last-of-its-kind grass bridge has spanned the river for 500 years—swaying in the breeze alongside a steel truss bridge built in 1968.

An Inca quipu

With such long distances to cover, travelers could use an efficient chain of way stations between Cuzco and the remote parts of the empire. At regular intervals, storehouses with stone walls and thatched roofs, called *tampu*, provided shelter and a place to stockpile food and trade items. Some of these buildings had room for llamas as well as people. Runners, called *chasquis*, were stationed along the roads about 6 to 9 kilometers (4 to 6 miles) apart. Their job was to relay information and keep it moving much faster than a single runner could. Since the Inca had no written language, the runners passed on memorized spoken messages, or used the *quipu*, a device made of strings which were knotted in patterns to represent numbers and other details. If there was trouble to report—a raid or invasion, for instance—runners lit a bonfire to alert the army. With this clever communication system, very little went on throughout the empire that was not soon known by the government in Cuzco.

Roads to Battle

Remains of the citadel in Cuzco

WHEN THE SPANIARDS first arrived in South America in 1532, they failed to understand the advantage the roads and landscape gave to the Inca armies. Runners could swiftly relay information about movements of enemy cavalry, allowing the Inca to choose the battleground, or prepare to ambush from a rugged hilltop where Spain's horses would be ineffective. But the Spanish realized they could take advantage of the elaborate road system to put down resistance, ransack cities, and tighten their control. Soon they had taken the city of Cuzco and had the upper hand.

The Spanish appointed an Inca man named Manco as emperor, allowing him to rule if he promised to do as they ordered. Instead, the emperor chose to leave the occupied city of Cuzco and rejoin the rebellious Inca forces gathering in the countryside. According to accounts written by Spanish storytellers, once plans of the Inca's preparations to recapture Cuzco were known, a small group of Spanish cavalry rode out to stop them. The Inca let them cross a river bridge and enter a narrow canyon. Less alert after a long ride in the thin mountain air, the cavalry were completely surprised by warriors hurling stones with rope slings. The mounted soldiers turned to flee, only to find the bridge gone. Trapped! Now the Inca played their final card: they pushed huge boulders from the heights, crushing their enemies in the ravine. They finished off any survivors with heavy clubs, and took the horses for their own use.

As long as the Inca used the landscape to their advantage, their assaults on the Spanish were effective. A time came, though, when the tables began to turn. In a decisive battle to take the city of Lima, the Inca faced the cavalry on open ground, their commander leading the attack as usual. But their leader was killed, and, badly outnumbered, the army lost its will to fight. The enemy soon wore down their resistance in other battles, and the Spanish conquest was complete by 1572.

The Inca Roads Endure

THE INCA EMPIRE IS NO MORE, but it has been long outlived by its roads. The Spaniards damaged some surfaces with their horses and wheeled carts. But many original roads have survived quite unchanged, especially those in less populated, mountainous regions. When explorers like the American Hiram Bingham began searching for legendary Inca ruins in the early 20th century, they followed the roads. It made sense to them that the ancient Inca would not have used such a huge amount of energy building roads unless they led to destinations of importance. Today, villagers in the Andes still travel these traditional pathways that link their communities and help them preserve their culture and customs.

But the intrusion of modern life—and the arrival of the automobile—has had a major impact. Some of the old roads were too steep or too remote for car travel, and new mountain routes were needed. The building of communications towers and power transmission lines, the growth of the mining industry, and the use of farm machinery like tractors have all affected parts of the road. But the fact that so much of the route is still intact—even if paved over—is a lasting testament to the wisdom and skill of Inca engineers.

Inca Trail to Machu Picchu

A four-day hike along a 45-kilometer (28-mile) road called the Inca Trail will take you to an astonishing place. Buried in jungle vegetation, the ancient city of Machu Picchu was unknown to outsiders for nearly 400 years, until local farmers led Hiram Bingham there in 1911. Once the jungle was cleared, about 200 houses and temples of precisely fitted, heavy granite rocks were revealed, along with complex irrigation systems and terraced farm fields. All of this had been built with few tools, but with a sophisticated understanding of scientific principles. Today, so many people want to see Machu Picchu's wonders that the Peruvian government has limited the number of visitors to protect this unique historic site.

KHYBER PASS

Valley of Invasions

NAME

The origin of the name is uncertain, but *khyber* is thought to mean "fort" or "castle" in Hebrew.

DESCRIPTION

This high pass winds through the Hindu Kush mountain range in the Himalayas. Sheer rocky cliffs hug the sides of the pass, which in some places is about as wide as four football fields. Elsewhere, the route runs through a valley five times that width. Throughout its length, the steep grades and tight hairpin turns slow travelers on the paved road.

AGE

As old as the Himalayas, the Khyber Pass may have been first used by large numbers of nomadic people migrating from Central to South Asia around 1500 BCE. It became part of an ancient trading network called the Silk Road.

Kabul •
Jalalabad •
Khyber Pass
Jamrud • •Peshawar
• Islamabad

AFGHANISTAN

PAKISTAN

INDIA

ARABIAN SEA

WHO USES IT NOW?

Since the 1980s, refugees from conflicts in Afghanistan have used the pass as an escape route, along with smugglers, drug traders, and tourists.

CLAIM TO FAME

The pass is a historical gateway from Central to South Asia, and a main link between Peshawar (Pakistan) and Kabul (Afghanistan). This important position means the pass has seen countless battles and is still the site of hostilities between warring factions in the surrounding countries.

Khyber Pass
2012

The road west from Peshawar is busier than Yasir expected. Cars, vans, and buses speed past the transport truck his dad is driving. The ride is anything but smooth over potholes and ruts in the pavement. It will be slower once they reach the Khyber Pass and drive toward Afghanistan. The load of wheat in the back of the truck is food aid from the United States. This morning, Yasir helped his father and the other men load the heavy sacks. They are anxious to complete the trip in daylight. But there is no guarantee they will make it through the pass today.

Along this dangerous route, with its long history of war, unpredictable events close the road from time to time. It might be an IED explosion or a rockslide. Then everyone trying to cross the border must wait, always for hours, sometimes for days. Yasir and his father have brought some food in case they have to sleep in the cab of the truck tonight.

Yasir gazes at the ruins of the stone-walled fort at Jamrud. He remembers learning that it was built by Sikhs in the early 1800s, and was the scene of battles with Afghan forces. This spot on the stony hills marks the entrance to the valley where their truck will follow a winding route between towering cliffs. Along the way, he'll watch for more relics—including the burned remains of NATO supply trucks left in 2008 after the U.S. war against the Taliban. At the highest point in the road, Landi Kotal, they'll drive past shops that sell smuggled weapons and drugs, hidden behind corrugated metal walls and concrete barriers on the road. Then, Yasir's dad will pull into the line of vehicles waiting to have documents checked by border security. For safety, he knows they must stay in the truck. If all goes well, they'll be in Kabul before dark.

Karakorum Highway, through the Khyber Pass

The Story of the Khyber Pass

On EVERY CONTINENT, mountain ranges divide the land. People can only get from one side of those steep, rugged barriers to the other through a pass. These gaps in the mountains often follow a river valley, and may be long or short, straight or winding. The top of the pass may be a flat area, useful for buildings such as border control stations (if the mountains form the boundary between countries) or rest stops. Throughout history, people have used passes to travel, to exchange goods or information with a neighboring country, or to invade another land. They have built roads, railways, and sometimes tunnels to complete the route.

The Khyber Pass, one of the best-known mountain passes in Asia, is a narrow road that penetrates the Hindu Kush mountain range, near the western end of the Himalayas. Creating a gateway from Central Asia to the Indian subcontinent, the Khyber Pass has seen many waves of human migration and the flow of highly prized trade. But because of its strategic location, it has, for centuries, also witnessed the turmoil of war. What stories could the rocky hillsides of this short route—like crossing the Golden Gate Bridge 15 times—tell of those life-and-death struggles?

Route to a New Land

The steep walls of the pass, shown in an illustration from around 1880

AMONG THE PEOPLE who have taken this route south were a large nomadic group called the Aryans, who funneled through the Khyber Pass from Europe and Central Asia in 1500 BCE. They settled as farmers in the fertile Indus River Valley, and others followed. The Persians invaded and controlled the northern plains (today, Afghanistan and Pakistan) from 530 BCE. Their reign ended 200 years later, when Alexander the Great, king of Macedon (now part of Greece), expanded his empire into India.

The Khyber Pass was a key link in a network of trading routes called the Silk Road. It connected many parts of the ancient world on land, and via sea routes on the Indian Ocean. Traders and merchants traveled in camel caravans as protection against thieves, exchanging goods like silk from China; spices, jewels, and textiles; paper and gunpowder (both invented in China); and porcelain. This movement of people also contributed to the spread of cultures, religions, and ideas. One group, the Kushan, who migrated from Central Asia along the trading network through the Khyber Pass, established their prosperous civilization in northern India in the third century CE, combining aspects of both Greek and Indian culture. They were followed by another empire, the Guptas, which flourished until the sixth century.

Later, in the 16th century, one of the world's greatest kingdoms, the Mughal Empire, spread the Islamic religion to the many diverse groups that lived in northern India by that time. But in the northwest, the Pashtun, a large ethnic group, rose against the authority of the Mughals in a civil war and won the prize of their homeland, called Afghanistan. Nestled against India's border, Afghanistan gave the Pashtun control of the western end of the Khyber Pass.

When European explorers found a sea route to the rich land of spices in the East, the Mughal Empire was threatened and weakened. By the 17th century, Britain's East India Company dominated its trading rivals from Portugal, Holland, and France. The British government then fought and overpowered southern Indian states to consolidate its authority in the region they renamed British India.

British Rule in Afghanistan

MEANWHILE, RUSSIA SAW how Britain had risen to global power largely due to its command of the seas. Russia's only useful seaport was far to the east, on the Pacific coast. But if it could open up a land route south to the Arabian Sea, it would have closer access to the most active trading areas of the world's oceans. To get to the Arabian Sea, though, it would have to go through Afghanistan. British leaders knew Russia was close enough to the Khyber Pass to follow in the footsteps of other invaders, which could pose a threat to

A map from the early 1900s shows red-coated British soldiers looking toward Afghanistan; the Khyber Pass is shown at right

Britain's prized possession, India. To prevent this, the British had to put their own leader in command in Afghanistan. Their invasion in 1839 resulted in great loss of life among Afghanistan's forces, which were much weaker. To maintain control during their occupation, the British changed the laws in ways that imposed economic hardship on Afghans. Afghans, meanwhile, began to fiercely resist how their country was being used in a political game between more powerful nations.

That growing unrest soon erupted into outright rebellion. Afghans laid siege to British encampments until, in January 1842, the remaining British fled in the frigid winter weather, attempting to escape through the Khyber Pass. Afghans waited in ambush, however, and the 4,500 troops and 12,000 civilians that had made up the British community in Afghanistan paid for Britain's aggression. Only one survivor made it back to India.

Defending the Pass

THE BRITISH WOULD RETURN to Afghanistan again in the late 1800s amid complicated political relationships in Europe. By this time, Germany had become an aggressive power with its sights set on India. And Russia saw yet another way to challenge Britain's dominance by taking India before Germany had a chance to do so. Naturally, the Khyber Pass would provide the best attack route. With a Russian invasion looming, and Afghanistan's refusal to accept Britain's advice or a military presence, in 1878 the British sent its invading army through the Khyber Pass once again. After numerous battles throughout Afghanistan in this Second Anglo–Afghan War, Britain forced the Afghans to give up control of the Khyber Pass. The scene of so many clashes, the pass had become a critical defense point for Britain's trade interests in India.

Afghan tribesmen serving British forces around 1878, during the Second Anglo–Afghan War

With security in mind, British engineers built a paved road shortly after the First World War (1914–18) to allow quick movement of soldiers if necessary. Then, in 1925, they finished construction of the Khyber Pass railway, running from a point near the Indian city of Peshawar to the border with Afghanistan. Fearing a German attack in the Second World War (1939–45), the British installed concrete fortifications called "dragon's teeth" to slow enemy tanks or force them to detour closer to the hillsides through the valley, where defensive weapons were mounted. With the defeat of Germany in 1945, that danger passed. But the Khyber Pass is still littered with signs of the hostilities that took place there, including remains of several forts and guard posts in the steep-sided valley.

FORTS IN THE KHYBER PASS

Through history, defensive fortifications were built at key points in the pass. At the eastern end, the fort built in 1823 at Jamrud was the scene of fighting during the First Anglo–Afghan War, from 1839–42. In 1878, during the Second Anglo–Afghan War, the fort of Ali Masjid and the cliffs nearby were held by 3,700 Afghans armed with only 34 guns, which they aimed at a British and Indian force of 12,000 men in a day-long battle. By the next morning, the outnumbered Afghan forces had withdrawn. Fort Maude is a present-day police post in the Federally Administered Tribal Areas (FATA) of the pass.

A New Master

In 1947, the Indian Independence Act established India and Pakistan as separate, self-governing nations within the British Commonwealth, ending British control. West Pakistan now controlled the Khyber Pass along Afghanistan's border. (East Pakistan was renamed Bangladesh in the 1970s, after the country was divided by civil war.) The mountainous lands on either side of the pass had long been home to local tribal clans run by warlords. Tensions persisted between ethnic groups in both India and Pakistan until they reached an impasse. Pakistan closed its border with India in 1961.

THE KHYBER PASS RAILWAY

The British-built Khyber Pass railway transported soldiers to the Afghan border and kept them supplied in times of war. When this challenging construction project was completed, it ran along the hillside overlooking the road, through 34 tunnels and over 94 bridges, to a station at the summit town of Landi Kotal. In 1982, the railway was closed as it had become more practical to move goods with trucks on the road. However, 10 years later, a private company restored the railway for tourism. It drew adventurous travelers until 2001, when the U.S. invasion and war in Afghanistan made it too dangerous. Although it was restarted a couple of years later, few came to ride it. Flood damage has since kept the tracks closed. In early 2015, Pakistan Railways began a study to see if at least part of it could be used again.

Russian soldiers take Afghan prisoners in 1987

That left Afghanistan looking for another trading channel. Russia was willing to provide it by building a tunnel to the north through the Hindu Kush mountains, steering clear of the Khyber Pass. By 1979, though, Russia had begun to move thousands of troops into the country; the occupation Britain had feared in the previous century was finally happening. Now the border with Pakistan became a strategic barrier against a new threat: Soviet Communism. And it soon became an escape route for several million Afghans who did not want to stay under Russian domination.

HIPPIE TRAIL

Beginning in the 1960s, traveling through Asia became a kind of pilgrimage for young people. There was a new interest—spiritual, cultural, musical—in India, Pakistan, Nepal, and neighboring countries. Adventure-seekers from Western countries traveled to Europe, then went by bus, car, or rail, or—the cheapest way—by hitchhiking from Turkey through the Middle East to Afghanistan. Because of the casual style of dress and long hair of these travelers, their route, which included the Khyber Pass, was called the "hippie trail." Many visitors knew Afghanistan primarily as a source for the popular drug hashish, as well as opium. For the next decade, Afghanistan welcomed foreign travelers to enjoy its easygoing lifestyle and developing prosperity. After the 1970s, however, social and political changes led to unrest in the country, and conflicts between religious groups created a tense and dangerous climate that intentionally discouraged foreigners.

Travelers along the "hippie trail" in 1975

Invasions from Two Sides

Under the Taliban, Afghan women were forced to wear a face-covering burka in public

HISTORY SEEMS to repeat itself for Afghanistan when it comes to occupation by other countries. By 1988, the Russians were forced to withdraw after years of war against Afghan groups who resented their presence. The Afghan government then found itself opposing growing militant forces within the country led by religious extremists. Money, weapons, and drugs were smuggled in as the country descended into its own internal war.

In the 1990s, a militant Muslim organization called the Taliban took control of the government. At first, they appeared to bring peace and order to the land, but the Taliban soon began to enforce a strict interpretation of Islamic laws (*sharia*) that became extremely oppressive, especially to women. Many Afghans, fearing for their lives, escaped across the border to Pakistan, just as others had fled from Russian occupation years earlier—once again through the Khyber Pass.

Then, radical forces supported by the Taliban began to organize attacks on Western targets. After the September 11, 2001, destruction of the World Trade Center in New York City, the United States took military action, sending troops to Afghanistan to crush the terrorist network known as al-Qaeda and remove the Taliban from power. The fighting sent a new flood of refugees into Pakistan, and along with them, suspected terrorists trying to evade capture.

Tensions still run high between the countries linked by the Khyber Pass. Although the Afghan government is now responsible for security in the country, some U.S. and NATO troops remain to help Afghanistan develop its own armed forces.

The Pass Today

THE KHYBER PASS, for so long a key player in the dramatic events between Afghanistan and India (and later Pakistan), remains a place where trouble might flare up at any time. The small town of Landi Kotal, at the summit near the Afghan border, is a haven for smugglers of weapons, drugs, and electronics. Still a trade route, now called the N-5 National Highway, the tightly controlled pass sees hundreds of trucks loaded with goods stop at military and police checkpoints at Torkham each day. Everyone is constantly on alert at this single legal crossing point between the countries.

The Torkham crossing point in 2016

The pass is usually closed at night, and signs alert the traveler that it might be shut down at any time—in case of attacks on supply vehicles or IED (improvised explosive device) explosions that occur without warning. Straying from the dangerous roadway might be even more perilous because there is little police presence in the tribal areas in the valley. And in winter, as the retreating British once discovered to their dismay, the road can be blocked by heavy snow and avalanches, or rock slides. But in spite of all the risks, today tourists are among the main invaders who trek through the legendary Khyber Pass, still playing a vital part in Asian history.

TRANS-SIBERIAN RAILWAY

Unifying a Nation

NAME

Also called Great Siberian Railway,
or the Trans-Siberian.

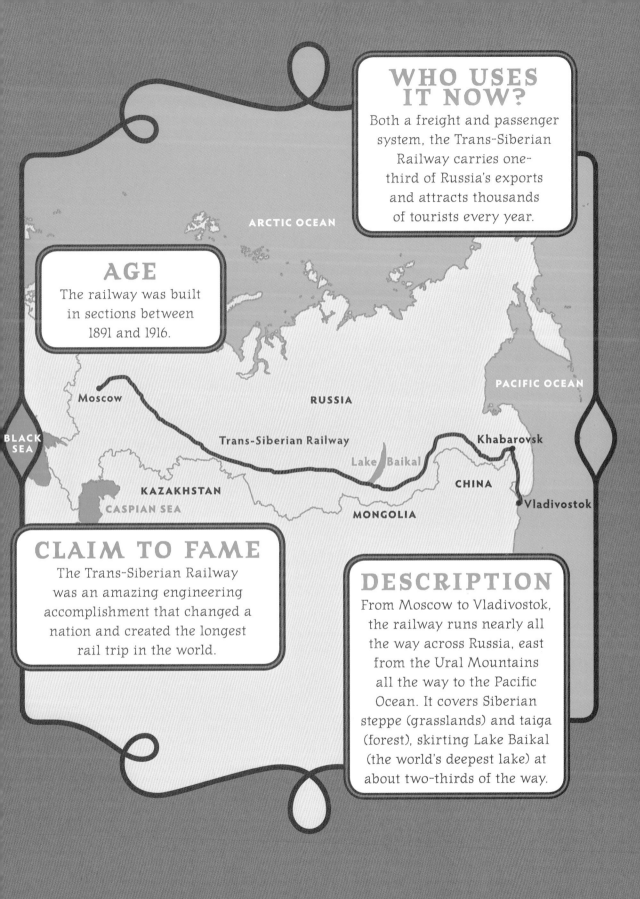

WHO USES IT NOW?

Both a freight and passenger system, the Trans-Siberian Railway carries one-third of Russia's exports and attracts thousands of tourists every year.

AGE

The railway was built in sections between 1891 and 1916.

ARCTIC OCEAN

PACIFIC OCEAN

Moscow

RUSSIA

BLACK SEA

Trans-Siberian Railway

Khabarovsk

Lake Baikal

CHINA

KAZAKHSTAN

Vladivostok

CASPIAN SEA

MONGOLIA

CLAIM TO FAME

The Trans-Siberian Railway was an amazing engineering accomplishment that changed a nation and created the longest rail trip in the world.

DESCRIPTION

From Moscow to Vladivostok, the railway runs nearly all the way across Russia, east from the Ural Mountains all the way to the Pacific Ocean. It covers Siberian steppe (grasslands) and taiga (forest), skirting Lake Baikal (the world's deepest lake) at about two-thirds of the way.

On the Trans-Siberian Railway late 1800s

Sofia's mother shakes her awake. It's still dark inside the rumbling railway car but bands of early daylight filter through gaps in the walls. Sofia stretches and sits up. She's cold, stiff, and sore from sleeping on the dusty wooden floor. Her throat is dry and her stomach tight with hunger. There is little bread and sausage left to share among the dozen families riding in this car into Siberia. Yesterday, after six days, her father said they must be almost halfway. Sofia wishes she could sleep the rest of the way to their destination.

She can feel the train slowing. Is it another of the endless delays because of an engine breakdown or a buckled section of this newly built track? Will they sit idle in the middle of nowhere for hours, not knowing what is going on? Or are they coming into one of the small stations dotted along the route? Then at least they'll be let out to line up at the samovar for hot water to make tea. They'll have to hurry, though. As soon as the steam engine takes on water from the huge tank beside the tracks, the train will move on again.

If Sofia had known how unbearable this journey would be, she would have begged her parents to stay home in the Ukraine. But the tsar has promised each family a small acreage so they can build a farm and grow food for the increasing Russian population. It's a new chance to make a living, even though this trip is taking every bit of money her father had saved. It is only possible because of the reduced fare offered to encourage peasant families like hers to move east into Siberia.

As the train stops with a shudder and screech of brakes, Sofia grips her father's hand and smiles up at him. She can see the hope in his eyes. In only a few more days, they will arrive at their new home.

Along the Trans-Siberian in late fall

The Story of the Trans-Siberian Railway

Can you imagine heading off on a train trip that today takes nine days and stretches across one-tenth of Earth's land surface—over grassland and permafrost, across mountains and rivers—moving through eight time zones? Now picture what it must have been like, in the late 1800s, to take on the tremendous challenge of building what many call the world's greatest railway: the Trans-Siberian.

An Isolated Land

Before Siberia came under the rule of Russian tsars in the 1600s, this land, which sprawls across northern Asia to meet the Arctic and Pacific Oceans, was populated by indigenous peoples largely descended from Asian tribes, as well as nomadic trappers and fur traders. Some Cossack explorers—from Russia and the Ukraine—traveled north as far as the Bering Strait. But the harsh climate and lack of safe roads or means of communication tempted few to venture into this remote region. The Russian population that developed after the ninth century, descended from Slavic peoples in Europe, lived mainly west of the Ural Mountains, close to European cities.

From 1648 until 1900, almost all the Russians in Siberia were sent there against their will. They were exiled criminals, sentenced to hard labor in silver, gold, and coal mines in the far-flung frozen territory. This population did not exactly create the kind of reputation that would encourage other Russians to make the move!

Siberian convicts, around 1885

Why Build a Railway?

ALTHOUGH SIBERIA REMAINED LARGELY ISOLATED and uninviting, Russia acquired the Pacific port city of Vladivostok from China in 1858, for its navy and for trade. That made the government think about how to use the rest of Russia's vast land and resources. How could they tie the immense country together from west to east?

The idea to build the Trans-Siberian Railway first arose in 1857. The governor general of Eastern Siberia envisioned how transportation between European Russia and Vladivostok could allow movement of trade goods, and provide a way to defend against possible invasions from China. But the idea did not get much support until Tsar Alexander III took the throne in 1881. The tsar realized that a rail line across Russia would encourage valuable trade with China and Japan, and even create closer ties to new American markets across the Pacific Ocean.

Siberia had another potential significance. By this time, European Russia's large and growing population needed more food. Siberian land could be opened up to farmers who would boost agricultural production. A railway was becoming an idea worth considering.

The Russian government had no money to invest in a railway, however. And it refused to use investments from foreign countries, fearing that might lead to foreigners winning political control. (Later, though, Russia did end up using American steel, and British money and skills.) Finding enough Russian funds was an ongoing problem that would both weaken the railway itself and threaten the tsar's command of his people.

The Railway Route

Work began in 1891 on a patchwork of rail lines. Sections of track were built at about the same time in both the eastern and the western regions. By 1900, once tracks extended from the east side of Lake Baikal, passengers could travel there from Moscow, take a ferry (which carried the whole train) across the lake, ride a combination of trains and river steamboats to Khabarovsk, and from there journey to Vladivostok.

A line to bypass the steamboat sections was too difficult and expensive because of permafrost (frozen ground that rarely thaws even in summer heat) and mountains requiring tunnels. So Russia reached an agreement with China in 1897 to build a shortcut through Manchuria, in northeastern China. Then, in 1904, a new railway line around Lake Baikal replaced the ferry, with over 200 trestles and bridges, and 33 tunnels. Those additions ironed out tricky sections. But it was not until 1916 that the last link, the Amur Railway, was finished, allowing passengers to travel all the way from Moscow to Vladivostok by train through Russian territory.

The route around Lake Baikal

Facing Tough Challenges

ONCE THE PROJECT BEGAN, the tsar demanded speedy construction, so work continued six days a week through the searing heat of summer. Flooding and landslides, hordes of black flies and mosquitoes, and outbreaks of cholera and plague tormented the workers through their 14 daily hours of labor, from dawn to dusk. When winter came, the shifts were shortened to eight hours, but there was no escape from the brutal cold, which could reach minus 50 degrees Celsius (minus 58 degrees Fahrenheit). Workers lived in tents in summer and in crude log cabins or wagons on the railway in winter. They ate one hearty meal of hot stew at midday. As if the daily working conditions weren't bad enough, in eastern areas, roaming tigers terrified work parties and bandits often attacked.

While building railway tracks across open grasslands may seem straightforward, the same could not be said about the rest of the route. Swamps riddled the steppe land, along with deep permafrost, rivers, thick evergreen forests, and mountainous areas. Tracks shifted and bent under the weight of heavy trains on wet, unstable ground. Derailments were common, and constant repairs slowed the work. How would material be brought to out-of-the-way work sites without adequate roads? Were local supplies available?

SWITCHING THE TRACKS

When trains from other railway lines tried to use the Trans-Siberian tracks, they came to a dead stop. Why? The Trans-Siberian's unusual rail width didn't match the rails used elsewhere. The Russian government did this on purpose, believing that stopping to adjust the wheels of rail cars entering the country would slow any possible invasions.

A railway station node, where the lines meet

Unfortunately, the forests that took so much time and expense to clear weren't always good sources of hardwood for the "sleepers" (wood laid across the rail bed to support rails). So lumber had to be brought from great distances, along with almost everything else needed for construction. Stone and gravel for the rail bed were transported on river barges and by horse-drawn cart or sled. Iron for the rails came from European Russia, or traveled a roundabout sea route from Britain or Poland to Vladivostok, then up rivers into the center of Siberia. In 1914, one shipment of metal parts was lost in the Indian Ocean, delaying bridge construction by two years.

With limited money, materials had to be bought for the lowest price, and only what was absolutely necessary was purchased. That meant skimping: laying track in tight curves, taking short-cuts up steep slopes, using cheaper iron for rails and thinner layers of stone in narrower rail beds to support them. Bridges were built of wood rather than longer-lasting metal. All these methods soon proved unwise. The railway needed repairs before it was even fully opened, and had to be rebuilt constantly afterward.

WHO BUILT THE RAILWAY?

With few qualified engineers and little skilled labor in Siberia—
hardly any local peasants were willing to do the work—railway
crews were brought from European Russia, Italy, Turkey, and China.
To meet the demand, as many as 14,000 criminals and political
prisoners exiled to Siberia got reduced sentences in exchange
for railway work. Once the construction material arrived, workers
had only hand tools, such as wooden shovels, axes, saws, and
wheelbarrows, to do their jobs. Throughout the 12-year-long
main phase of the building project, finding enough labor was as
constant and serious a problem as finding money to pay for the
construction. In total, up to 90,000 people worked on the railway.

Prisoners at work on
the railway in 1894

A settlement along the Trans-Siberian Railway

Russians Head East

Even on "completed" sections, the work was by no means finished. When the first passengers rode the rails in 1896, delays and breakdowns were common on the two-week-long, uncomfortable journey. Coal used for fuel was often stolen. Trains ran slowly over unstable tracks, some laid directly across river ice if bridges were unfinished; passengers sometimes had to walk across the ice in case the heavy train broke through it. Food service was often available only at small stations, unless you were in one of the luxury cars that carried those who could afford it. But in spite of all these drawbacks, in its first 10 years the Trans-Siberian carried over a million people into Siberia and was already transforming Russia.

A group of new arrivals in Siberia, around 1910

From start to finish and beyond, the Trans-Siberian played many roles in the growth of the country. The government had one major goal: migration. To encourage people to leave overcrowded European Russia, with its chronic shortages of food, the government offered to help pay for rail travel and the costs of building homes on free plots of land in Siberia. This was an exciting opportunity for those seeking to escape Russia's historic serf system, in which all profits from their labor went to the government. Far from St. Petersburg, the center of government, people could live in a freer society, farming and selling much-needed food (butter, wheat, rye, and meat) back to the west. Up to 15,000 a week took the train on a one-way trip east until, by 1914, three million people lived in Siberia, making it a thriving industrial and agricultural part of the country. Settlements popped up on a wide strip on either side of the railway, where smaller branch lines extended farther out. The full journey from Moscow to Vladivostok now took only nine days.

More Trouble Ahead

WHILE THE NEW TSAR, Nicholas II, was pouring money into costly railway construction and an unsuccessful war with Japan far to the east, political parties had begun to stir up the hungry population against his unlimited power. Reforms—including more freedom of speech, the right to belong to political groups, and the parliamentary elections of 1905— were not enough to satisfy discontented Russians, who now saw their tsar as a leader out of touch with ordinary people. A working-class party called the Bolsheviks fanned those growing flames of unrest.

When Russia entered the First World War in 1914 on the side of the Allies (Britain and France), the Trans-Siberian became a vital route for bringing soldiers and resources into Europe from Vladivostok. Once again, the poor condition of the railway and a shortage of rail cars and locomotives made it difficult to transport goods and supplies to bolster the fight against Germany. And after suffering losses of over 250,000 in early battles, Russian soldiers began to retreat and desert.

Tsar Nicholas II

The Bolsheviks, led by Vladimir Lenin, gained supporters by promising to take Russia out of the war and rebuild the country's industry and agriculture. Finally, in 1917, the tsar abdicated (gave up his position as ruler). Within a few months, Lenin's promise of "peace, bread, and land" became the rallying cry for an uprising.

In what was called the October Revolution, the Red Army (controlled by the Bolsheviks) and the White Guard (the forces of the government) clashed over an important prize: control of the Trans-Siberian Railway. Amid all the fighting, many bridges, stations, and water towers were destroyed.

A Railway Across Canada

Six years before Russia began its ambitious rail project, the Canadian Pacific Railway, running across the country from Montreal to the West Coast, was completed. It was built in just four years, between 1881 and 1885, in part using around 15,000 hired workers from China, who worked in harsh conditions. Both ventures faced similar geographical challenges, such as mountains and rugged northern landscapes with peat bogs and vast expanses of rock. Like Russia, Canada built its railway to unify the country and bring settlers to its underpopulated and undeveloped regions.

A Canadian Pacific train traveling through the Rocky Mountains

Then, in 1918, struggling Bolshevik revolutionaries made the drastic decision to execute Tsar Nicholas II and his family, ending the rule of emperors in Russia that had begun with Peter the Great in 1696. This action set off a long and violent civil war. The Bolsheviks triumphed in 1920, becoming the Communist Party and renaming the country the United Soviet Socialist Republic (USSR). Joseph Stalin, who succeeded Lenin as leader, began a series of "five-year plans" to modernize Russian industry and agriculture, at the same time ruthlessly suppressing all opposition.

During the Second World War, Stalin used the Trans-Siberian railway to transport Allied reinforcements to the Western Front as well as to remove industrial equipment, such as expensive locomotives, to Siberian locations, safely out of Nazi hands.

In the 1950s and '60s, cities continued to grow along the Trans-Siberian as oil and gas resources were developed in northern Siberia. Today, freight moves faster to Russian ports by rail than by sea, and the impact of equipment failure or weather delays is quickly felt. The Trans-Siberian Railway has changed the face of Russia, becoming one of the most heavily used rail systems in the world.

STALIN'S GULAGS

In the 1920s and '30s, Stalin organized huge collective farms, taking control of land from individual owners in order to efficiently increase food production and control prices. But the farmers whose small plots were taken over by the government resented the loss of their land and freedoms. In factories, Stalin set strict production targets that many of the poorly paid workers found impossible to meet, and strikers openly defied the government. For millions of these protesters opposition meant exile, via the Trans-Siberian, to forced-labor camps in Siberia, called gulags. Those who avoided execution and survived torture were put to work in mines and factories, or forced to build roads and railways.

7

CHILKOOT TRAIL

Rough Road to Riches

NAME

Named for a Tlingit First Nations clan indigenous to the Alaska coast; Chilkoot also means "big fish." The trail was nicknamed in news reports "the meanest 32 miles in Alaska and British Columbia."

AGE

The Tlingit used the Chilkoot Trail for thousands of years to travel and trade.

WHO USES IT NOW?

Hikers with permits can follow the Chilkoot Trail in the Klondike Gold Rush International Historical Park, created in 1998 on the 100th anniversary of the Gold Rush.

ALASKA   YUKON

• Dawson City

Yukon River

• Whitehorse
• Lake Bennett
Dyea • Chilkoot Trail

GULF OF ALASKA

BRITISH COLUMBIA

DESCRIPTION

The Chilkoot Trail runs through a natural gap in Alaska's Coast Mountains, from the Pacific coast to Lake Bennett in Canada. The summit at Chilkoot Pass is 1,080 meters (3,550 feet) high, and marks the border between the United States and Canada. From the trail's end point, a long route down the Yukon River leads to the Klondike goldfields.

CLAIM TO FAME

This short, remote trail saw up to 40,000 gold seekers risk everything to chase dreams of striking it rich.

On the Chilkoot Trail
1897

Millie climbs onto the bench beside her mother and settles in for
another bumpy wagon ride. Cold rain drips from her hat. Good thing
the muddy, rutted trail from Dyea, where the two of them live in a
one-room cabin, to Canyon City is only a few miles. That's as close
as their horses can get to the steep approach to Chilkoot Pass. Then
they'll turn the wagon around and head back to pick up more goods.

Her mother shakes the reins, and the two horses strain into their
harness. This load is heavy, but that means more money for their one-
wagon freight operation. In the few weeks since they started hauling
stampeders' outfits, they've been making a good profit, charging one
and a half cents a pound. Millie is proud of her mother for working
hard to provide for them in this chaotic place.

When they'd arrived on the ship with hundreds of gold seekers in the
summer, Millie worried that their meager savings would not last long,
and they'd have to take the next ship back to Vancouver before winter.
But she'd underestimated her mom's determination, and the appeal of
her cooking to these stampeders—mostly men—so far from home.

First Mom had baked biscuits, which Millie had helped to sell, hot,
by the dozen. Then Mom took on an extra job cooking at the newly built
hotel until she earned enough to buy this freight business. It might only
last a few months, until the rush of the stampede ends, but it pays well
enough that they'll be able to set up their own bakery shop to carry on.

Millie is looking forward to working indoors again, especially
on days like this. She's glad she doesn't have to climb the steep
and dangerous trail, or head off into the wilderness to dig for gold.
Her family's gold will be found right here in town.

Packers climbing the "Golden Stairs" of the Chilkoot Pass in 1898

The Story of the Chilkoot Trail

Your feet are lumps of ice, your fingers numb. The biting wind and freezing temperatures snatch your breath away. Your back aches from lugging a sack of oatmeal as heavy as a cocker spaniel. Tread the uneven, icy steps carefully or you'll bump into the climber ahead of you, and maybe lose your balance. No one will stop. They'll tramp right past, their only goal to reach the top of this miserable mountain, unload their pack, and then do it all over again, and again...

Luckily, a photographer took a picture of this famous 1898 scene on a notorious part of the Chilkoot Trail. Otherwise it might be hard to believe it really happened. Like links in a human chain, tens of thousands of men and hundreds of women toiled up the long, steep slope carrying the supplies they needed to spend months mining for gold. They had left families, jobs, and everything they owned behind to chase

Panning for gold

the golden nuggets that danced in their dreams. Few actually found any riches. Many died trying. What drove all these people to become part of that life-changing event, the Great Klondike Gold Rush?

Why the Rush for Gold?

GOLD—BEAUTIFUL, WARM, an emblem of wealth and luxury—has attracted people throughout history, not just for its appearance, but for its trading value. It was so important as a symbol of wealth and a secure economy that in the 1800s some countries made it government policy to allow the exchange of printed money for a fixed amount of gold. They called this rule the "gold standard." But in the 1890s, people in the United States became worried about the value of their currency, and many began to exchange dollars for gold. Soon the government's supply of gold ran low, and because the dollar was tied to the gold standard, without gold the government could not print more money. With less money available, the slow economy turned into a full-fledged depression in 1893. People lost jobs, homes, and farmland. The kind of help available in times of financial trouble today—food banks, unemployment insurance—did not exist in those days. Families starved.

The world needed more gold! The timing of a huge discovery in the Klondike seemed like a miracle. With high hopes, but without knowing much about conditions in the north or even about gold mining, more than 100,000 "stampeders" from all over the world rushed to the goldfields. Those with no jobs hoped luck would help them find enough wealth to buy homes and feed their families. Many saw an opportunity to prove they could succeed by their own hard work, rather than toiling for a demanding factory boss. Some walked away from good jobs, lured by a sense of adventure and the chance to explore a new frontier.

Where Was the Gold?

THE LAND WHERE GOLD WAS FOUND had been home to the indigenous people called the Tlingit for thousands of years. Theirs was a strong and well-established culture. They fished for salmon, halibut, and herring along the Alaska coast, and hunted deer, mountain goats, and birds in the rainforest and mountains. They crossed the mountains to trade with indigenous peoples in the Yukon interior for lynx and fox furs, moose and caribou hides, beaver pelts, and copper. Tlingit clans controlled five mountain routes, but mainly used the Chilkoot Pass. When the first gold prospectors showed up in the 1880s, the Tlingit agreed to guide them on the trail through the pass.

Prospector George Carmack and his partners, Skookum Jim and Dawson Charlie, made the big strike on Rabbit Creek (later renamed Bonanza Creek) in August of 1896. But the world didn't hear of it until the following summer, when steamships arrived in Seattle and San Francisco carrying "tons of gold," worth $1.5 million. Immediately people raced to buy their ticket on ships heading north to the Klondike.

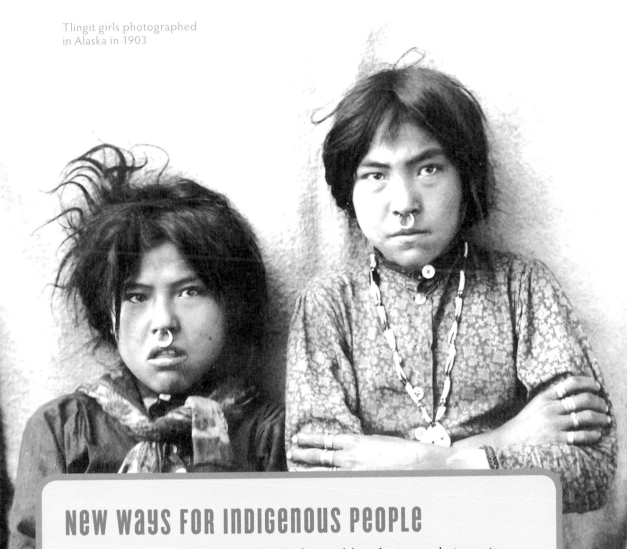

Tlingit girls photographed in Alaska in 1903

New Ways for Indigenous People

When the Tlingit agreed to guide the first gold seekers into their territory, they could not have imagined how their lives would change. During the Klondike Gold Rush, stampeders paid local indigenous people to carry their equipment over the Chilkoot Trail and supply them with firewood and food—salmon, moose, and caribou. However, that small income was overshadowed by serious and lasting damage. Prospectors dug along waterways, polluted water by washing gold ore in salmon streams, cut down forests for lumber, and hunted animals. Indigenous people were displaced from their land by more permanent settlement in the north. And new laws and customs, diseases, and discrimination brought profound social and cultural changes to the previously isolated indigenous communities.

Going Prepared

Stampeders preparing to board the ships pondered the advice of those who had returned from the gold strike. They were warned to take enough supplies—food, clothing, tents, bedding, and tools—to last a year, since in the Klondike, they would find only water and the wood they'd need for heat and building a shelter. Concerned for everyone's safety, the Royal North-West Mounted Police set up a Canadian customs post at the summit of the pass to turn back anyone ignoring that advice. Departure cities like Seattle, Vancouver, and Victoria became prosperous hives of commercial activity as everyone scrambled to buy what they needed for the trip.

THE SUPPLY LIST

To survive for a year in the northern wilderness, here were some of the things a stampeder needed:

- **flour** (180 kg/400 pounds)
- **beans** (45 kg/100 pounds)
- **dried apples, peaches, and apricots** (11 kg/25 pounds)
- **coffee** (11 kg/25 pounds)
- **5 bars of laundry soap**
- **60 boxes of matches**
- **warm clothes**
- **mosquito nets**
- **tools, frying pans, shovels, coffeepots, nails**
- **...and, of course, a gold pan!**

Many items quickly proved too heavy to carry; iron stoves, wheelbarrows, trunks, and even guns ended up dumped beside the trail.

A group with their supplies near Dyea Canyon

The cost of supplies was only the beginning. Shipping charges were calculated by weight. At an average of 900 kilograms (2,000 pounds) per person, a prospector's equipment was about half as heavy as a medium-sized car. On arrival at Dyea, a small town in Alaska of about 1,000 people, the steamships unloaded boxes, crates, and barrels onto barges, or right into the shallow water, since there was no dock. On shore, stampeders had to sort through a colossal pile to find their things, then cart them to higher, drier ground where they could pitch a tent. That would be their home until they were ready to start out on the Chilkoot Trail.

Most stampeders waited for snow to cover the loose rocks that made the trail especially susceptible to slides. But when they did, they traded warmer weather for brutally icy winter winds on the ascent. Wagons or packhorses (for a fee) transported their baggage the short distance to where the canyon narrowed to a footpath. Then they had to carry their own, or hire people called packers to move their things along the trail.

The Grueling Hike

A poster for an 1897 play about the Gold Rush

SHEEP CAMP was the last forested area to camp in before tackling the steep, rocky Long Hill. Stampeders edged fearfully past huge glaciers to the Scales, a treacherous hollow filled with ankle-turning boulders. But worse was yet to come, and many turned back, cured of their "gold fever" as soon as they saw it. Those brave enough to carry on faced the Golden Stairs, about 1,500 rough steps carved into the snow and ice, which was up to 10 meters (33 feet) deep. Part of the grade was so sheer you could easily touch the icy wall ahead while standing straight up! Better to keep your eyes on the slippery steps, and your right hand on a guide rope stretched from top to bottom. Every 20 steps or so, rest stops were dug into the snow. At the top, stampeders would stash their goods under a tarp, then—since their supplies were much too heavy to carry on their backs in one trip—head straight back down for another load. It might take an hour to climb up, but only a few minutes to toboggan down in a slick channel alongside the stairs. Imagine making more than 20 trips over this leg of the trail—like climbing the stairs in a 10-story building each time—while backpacking as much weight as possible!

GOLD RUSHES AROUND THE WORLD

CALIFORNIA, 1848–1855

With news of a big strike in 1848, over 300,000 gold seekers from around the world converged by land and sea on California—a U.S. territory newly acquired from Mexico. Many more joined the chase in the following year, earning the nickname "forty-niners." California goldfields yielded around $600 million worth of gold (worth $18 billion today) and San Francisco grew into a booming port city. That wealth led to California becoming a state in 1850. But unlike in the Klondike, there were few laws in place, so miners made their own rules in the rough "Wild West."

AUSTRALIA, 1855 AND 1890

Gold discoveries in southeastern Australia in the 1850s drew over 370,000 prospectors, or "diggers," mainly from England. They soon outnumbered the convicts who had been sent to settle the country in the late 1700s. As there was no single trail leading to gold sites— some of them were on sheep ranches—the government controlled operations by selling licenses to dig deep underground. The rush fueled the economies in established towns and led to railways being built.

SOUTH AFRICA, 1886

Diamonds, then gold, brought a rush of prospectors to South Africa in the late 1800s. Starting in 1867, millions were made from mining diamonds at great depths using a workforce of poorly paid, cruelly treated black South Africans. Then gold was discovered, but unlike in the Klondike, where it could be scooped from a stream by anyone with a pan, in South Africa it lay buried in deep, twisting tunnels. Wealthy white mine owners controlled the mines and the profits.

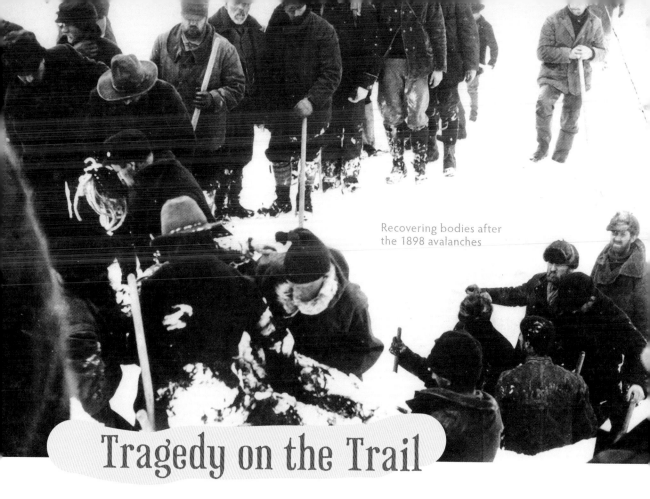

Recovering bodies after the 1898 avalanches

Tragedy on the Trail

Day after winter day, through frigid temperatures and blizzards, stampeders struggled over the trail. Warmer spring winds began to trigger small slides from glaciers burdened with huge loads of fresh snow. Packers noted the dire warning and refused to hike above Sheep Camp. The previous September, a dam of glacier ice had let go, sending floodwater, boulders, and trees smashing through the camp. Fortunately, only one person was killed. Then, on April 3, 1898, the roar of three avalanches thundering down the slope sent climbers racing for their lives. But the snow surged faster; it caught, tumbled, and buried dozens. Searchers dug frantically for days to save the many people whose voices could be heard beneath the snow shouting for help. The march up the trail carried on, though some bodies were not recovered until the snow melted that summer. The Slide Cemetery at Dyea is the final resting place for 50 of the 70 or so who died.

HARD TIMES FOR HORSES, TOO

Facing the task of carrying a ton of supplies over a long, treacherous trail, some stampeders tried using packhorses. Sold at bargain prices, and in bad shape to begin with, they were shipped north and often dumped over the side in Dyea harbor to swim to shore. The poor treatment continued along the trail. A fallen horse might be dragged to the top, or slid down to the bottom. Bodies of horses that had slipped or broken their legs on the rocks littered the trail; others too worn out to carry on were shot or turned loose. Many starved because their own food was too heavy to carry. Stories told of horses exhausted to the point of collapse appearing to deliberately walk off a ledge to their deaths. At least 3,000 horses died on the nearby White Pass trail, a longer route to Lake Bennett from Skagway. Sled dogs had it easier, since they were able to share human food and the shelter of a tent at night. If they couldn't climb the steps, they were carried on stampeders' backs.

Reaching the summit was only a partial victory. After the North-West Mounted Police inspected their equipment, stampeders continued past lakes and marshes and across narrow mountain ledges to frozen Lindeman and Bennett Lakes. There, they spent the winter building boats with wood from the surrounding forests. Once the ice broke up in spring, they could float the rest of the way to the Klondike in their overloaded boats, facing more dangers, including rapids.

savvy businesswomen

Women dreamed of riches during the gold rush, too. Some came with their husbands, but others, like Harriet Pullen, chose to go it alone. The single mother used her cooking skills (she sold apple pies) and knowledge of horses (she drove a freight wagon) to earn her way to hotel ownership. Another entrepreneur, Belinda Mulrooney, wisely anticipated the needs of stampeders by taking along $5,000 worth of clothing and hot water bottles, which she sold for $30,000. But her most famous achievement was the elaborate Fairview Hotel, furnished with brass beds and chandeliers, using electricity generated by a boat engine.

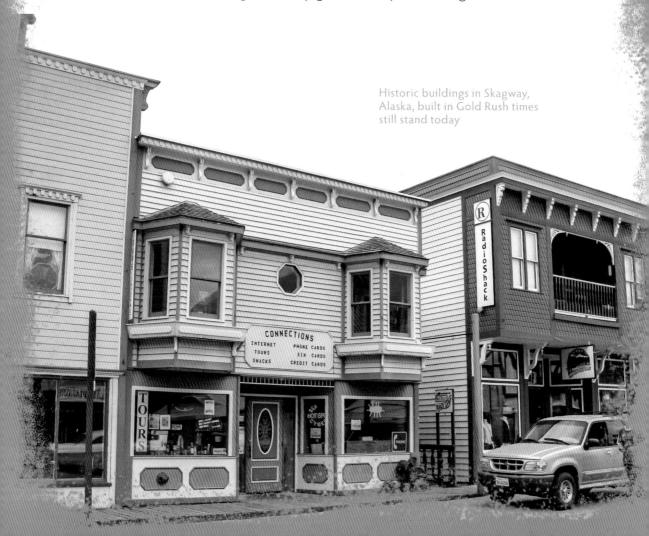

Historic buildings in Skagway, Alaska, built in Gold Rush times still stand today

Using Skills for Success

A modern hiker on the Chilkoot Trail

By the summer of 1898, between 30,000 and 40,000 people had tramped the Chilkoot Trail and spread out in search of gold. In fact, few found it, apart from the original prospectors whose lucky strike had started the whole business. But wealth came to many in other ways.

While the challenges proved too much for some, those who didn't give in and go home saw opportunity instead in the huge demand for services. Many more people found their fortune by building stores, or running hotels and banks, than by striking gold. At the same time, they established communities and transportation systems—like the White Pass & Yukon Route Railway built at Skagway—that were the basis of a new economy.

The Klondike Gold Rush was over by the end of 1899, but not before almost $12 million worth of gold had been mined—an astounding amount that enriched the world's economies. Today, the Chilkoot Trail still tempts hikers curious about that tumultuous era. And the lure of riches still draws a hopeful few to the goldfields to seek the elusive nuggets.

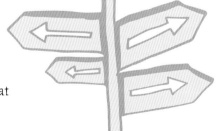

8

SERENGETI MIGRATION TRAIL

Nature Leads the Way

NAME
From the Maasai language (called Maa),
serengeti means "endless plains."

AGE

Home to wildlife for millions of years, and to Maasai herders since the 17th century.

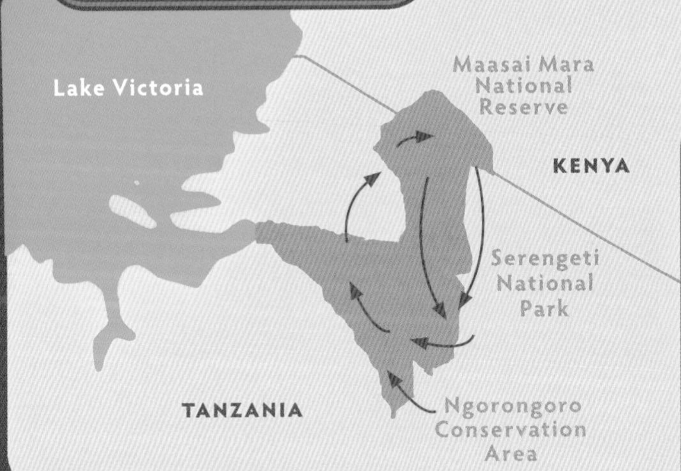

Lake Victoria

Maasai Mara National Reserve

KENYA

Serengeti National Park

TANZANIA

Ngorongoro Conservation Area

CLAIM TO FAME

The Serengeti is the site of the world's greatest migration of mammals, and is known for its incredible diversity of wildlife. It became a protected area in 1941, a National Park 10 years later, and a UNESCO World Heritage Site in 1979.

WHO USES IT NOW?

Over 300,000 tourists visit the Serengeti each year. Maasai living near Ngorongoro Crater graze and water their cattle there, but can no longer live inside the conservation area.

DESCRIPTION

Serengeti National Park is enormous—almost the size of the state of Hawaii. Located in Tanzania, just south of Kenya, its landscape includes grassland plains, savanna (grass with scattered shrubs and trees), and wooded areas. Together with the Ngorongoro Conservation Area to the southeast, it makes up the Serengeti-Ngorongoro Biosphere Reserve, established in 1981.

Ngorongoro Crater 1950s

The blood-red sun rises above the rim of the crater. Morning light floods across the land, stirring songbirds from nearby trees into flight. It is time for Lembui and his brothers to move the family's cattle out of the kraal, through the protective acacia fence that circles the huts. For the rest of the day, they will follow the herd as the animals graze the surrounding grasslands. Each boy carries a long walking stick to help prod the cattle along, keeping them together and safe from predators. Lembui knows there could be lions lurking in the shrubs and long grass, and he keeps a sharp lookout.

Across the savanna, he can see other Maasai families tending their herds, too. This pasture is becoming more crowded. Lembui knows it will get worse if the government goes ahead with its new idea to set aside special places where wildebeests, antelopes, zebras, giraffes, and elephants can be protected from hunters. The reserves will be centered around watering areas—fine for the wild animals, Lembui thinks, but not so good for Maasai people. Where will they water their herds? His father says the smaller pastures left to them will soon become overgrazed. Some families have been urged to take up farming. Then both the land and the cattle will suffer. It has never been the Maasai way to harm the land. Rather, they've always moved to new grazing areas to allow a pasture to recover.

But things are changing. There's even talk of Lembui and his brothers having to attend a school. That is not the Maasai way, either. He knows the elders are afraid traditions will be lost, especially if the young people learn new skills and take up different ways. Lembui is curious about learning to read. For now, though, he must look after the prize possessions of his family—their cattle—and bring them safely back to shelter by nightfall.

Wildebeests at Ngorongoro Crater

The Story of the Serengeti

THE ARRIVAL OF AUTUMN in the northern hemisphere triggers a southward journey for flocks of songbirds and geese in their long V formations. Salmon swim upstream in rivers to lay eggs for the next generation that will migrate to the sea. Mountain-dwelling animals move up and down the slopes as weather conditions affect their food and shelter. All of these migrations are responses to a need for a change in habitat. Some animals will travel record-setting distances to meet those needs; others, not so far. One amazing migration, near the equator in Africa, is relatively short in distance but attracts worldwide attention for the astonishing number of animals involved.

In an ancient land of towering mountains, vast grasslands, fertile valleys, and volcanic craters where the earliest humans left their footprints 3.6 million years ago, an incredible spectacle unfolds with the cycle of the seasons. It's called the largest migration of mammals anywhere on the planet. Enormous herds of wildebeests, zebras, and antelopes move through Serengeti National Park in the east African country of Tanzania. This journey has been going on for millennia. When human hunter-gatherers and herders came to live in the same territory at least 3,000 years ago, some closely followed the route of the animals. As the wildlife met its need for food, the nomadic people found the requirements of their distinctive lifestyle, too. One group, the Maasai, copied the annual passage of animals across the Serengeti while keeping watch over their grazing cattle.

How did the journeys of wildlife and humans become so interwoven in this place? And how do they now rely on each other for the survival of their way of life?

THE LION HUNT

A ritual lion hunt, called *olamayio*, was traditionally part of a coming-of-age ceremony, allowing young Maasai men to show their bravery and skill. At dawn, the warriors would stalk a lion by following its tracks, watching for droppings, or noticing where vultures circled above a recent lion kill. Hunters preferred to find a lion in the open, giving it a fair chance to challenge them. Pictures of Maasai warriors often show them holding a spear, the only weapon used to kill the lion. A successful hunt brought excitement to the family and honor to the hunter. Today, the Kenyan government allows the Maasai to kill only lions that have attacked their herds of livestock, or that threaten the community.

Ngorongoro Crater

Migration of Millions

It's early spring on the plains around Ngorongoro Crater, just southeast of the Serengeti. In the course of a few weeks, up to half a million wildebeest calves will stagger to their feet only moments after birth, ready to run. These newborns add their numbers to a herd already over a million animals strong. Plentiful grasses grow in the rich soil surrounding the old volcano, nourishing the enormous herd. According to fossil finds, this area, covered in short grass that makes it difficult for predators to hide, has been the primary site of wildebeest births for a million years. Once the dry season begins in June, though, the grass withers and dies, and the animals must move on to survive.

Archaeologists have found ancient cave paintings that depict the herd's rambling route north through a wetter area now called Serengeti National Park. By September, the animals reach Maasai Mara National Reserve in Kenya. Zebras lead the parade, eating the tops off the newly grown long grass, uncovering a banquet of other lush grasses and leaves that wildebeests relish. Smaller antelopes follow to munch on the shortest plants. In all, over 2.5 million animals are on the move.

The wildebeest migration begins

But the grazers are not alone on this migration route. Crocodiles lurk in the rivers that the herds must cross on their journey of several months. And as they travel through the home territories of some of Africa's largest predators, the lions, cheetahs, leopards, and hyenas are hungry to make a meal of them. Tall grasses that supply food also conceal these hunters, who have young of their own to feed. So Nature times lion births, for instance, to match the passage of the herds, when food will be plentiful.

The dry season triggers the trek north, but the coming of the annual rains in December draws the animals south again. Well-nourished from several months of grazing, the herds drift back to their starting point—Ngorongoro Crater. The grass restored by the rains will welcome the next spring's new generation, ensuring the eternal life cycle is repeated across "the endless plain"—the Serengeti. This massive movement of grazing animals determines the existence and future of all the area's wildlife.

The Maasai Journey

Besides wild creatures, people follow this historic route. Nomadic Maasai herders settled in Kenya in the 17th century and spread into Tanzania over the next 200 years. They preferred the open areas around Ngorongoro Crater for their herds of cattle; in the woodlands to the west, the disease-carrying tsetse fly and ticks made it impossible for humans to live there. The richness of the savanna allowed them to thrive, and a nearby mountain, Ol Doinyo Lengai, which means "Mountain of God" in the Maasai language, is sacred in their culture. The Maasai tended the cattle they depended on, regularly moving them to fresh grazing land and keeping them safe from predators. And as the rains dictated, they followed the growth of grass along with the wild herds, migrating north until the change of seasons brought them back through the Serengeti to Ngorongoro.

In this way, the Maasai respected their environment. No land was cultivated, nor was it overgrazed—it was left to renew itself for future use. The people lived mostly in harmony with the wild animals. Even with their reputation as brave warriors, the Maasai hunted lions only if cattle were attacked, or as part of an ancient coming-of-age ceremony for young men.

But in 1889, an infectious disease called rinderpest killed not only huge numbers of cattle but also wildlife such as buffalos, giraffes, and wildebeests. The loss of cattle was especially devastating to the Maasai, and without their food source, many died. To make matters worse, smallpox raged through the remaining population, killing many more people. Then Nature added one more blow: locusts moved in to strip the land of grass. It would take the Maasai over a decade to recover from the times of starvation and rebuild their population.

Wealth in Cattle

Cattle gave the Maasai everything they needed to survive. Cows provided milk and blood—harmlessly taken from a vein in the neck—both basic foods. Their meat was sometimes eaten at feasts as part of cultural ceremonies. Droppings, or dung, were spread over the huts to cement together the mud, sticks, and grass. Skins might become bedding. When a Maasai man chose a bride, he would pay for her with cattle.

Cattle were a family's wealth, so Maasai boys learned the responsibility of herding and tending them during the day. At night, they were kept inside the *kraal*, the space within a circle of huts surrounded by a thorny hedge of acacia branches, to keep them safe from attacks by lions.

Creating Parks

MEANWHILE, European missionaries and explorers began to take an interest in Africa's interior in the late 1800s, and settlers found the traditional Maasai lands all but empty of people. Wild game was still plentiful, though, so during the early 1900s, wealthy hunters on organized safaris made the most of the chance to take "trophy animals." In the years following the Second World War, poaching of animal skins and elephant ivory became recognized as a widespread problem. How long could animal populations keep up with such losses? Black rhinos, for example, are now categorized as critically endangered.

As part of the solution, in the mid-1940s the British, who were then governing Tanzania, began to set land aside for national parks and reserves in the region now known as Serengeti National Park. And the government in neighboring Kenya created a national reserve to protect the area that massive migrating herds of animals still use as their northern destination.

Ivory tusks from elephants are prized by poachers

Changes for the Maasai

Maasai share their limited water sources with wildlife, like these zebras

WHAT WAS GOOD for wildlife, though, did not prove to be favorable to the Maasai. New land use policies in the 1920s led to the creation of tribal reserves in semi-arid (or dry) areas. The best land went to farmers. Then, because of new park boundaries that took in more of their grazing land, the Maasai found their access to water was limited, their remaining land was soon overgrazed, and their nomadic traditions were restricted. At first, some Maasai were allowed to continue using park land, but as their population increased, conservation authorities argued their cattle were competing with wildlife for food and water. Since conservation and promotion of tourism were given top priority, in 1974 the Maasai were forced to live outside the Ngorongoro Conservation Area. Consequently, many Maasai had to reduce the size of their cattle herds, and could no longer move freely.

The Maasai's traditional territory became part of the national park system, but they were not compensated for the loss of land they had considered theirs by right. Because of their historical knowledge, they wanted a say, at least, in how the land would be managed. Instead, they were expected to break with centuries of tradition and become farmers, while their children would attend school.

About half a million Maasai now live mainly in Kenya. They sell products from their cattle, sheep, and goats in the cities to buy

A young Maasai herder with his goats in 2014

clothing and grain, and to pay to send their children to school. Some work as teachers or doctors, and more and more young Maasai are speaking up as activists on environmental concerns. The change has not come easily, especially to many older Maasai, who are devastated by the loss of their way of life. Their culture was founded on the belief that cattle were all-important, and that it was their duty to tend the herds. However, a new generation has begun to learn about their rights so they can make claims for land and share profits from its resources. Today, the tall, proud Maasai warriors who pose for tourist photos—wearing red blankets and with ochre staining their skin—represent this African heritage. But the knowledge gained from centuries of following migration routes through the Serengeti will soon be only told in stories, passed down through the memories of Maasai elders.

CARIBOU AND THE INUIT

The Great Migration in Africa's Serengeti has the largest numbers, but another movement of land mammals claims to cover the longest route—over 4,800 km (3,000 miles) every year. In Canada's far north, caribou head to the coastal plains in spring to calve, then graze on tundra plants all summer. The approach of winter's bitter cold drives them to shelter south of the treeline, digging for lichens in the soft, deep snow. Archaeological evidence shows that the annual round-trip journey dates back 27,000 years. The Maasai learned to follow the seasonal migration of Serengeti grazers, but rarely hunted them. However, Inuit in the Arctic have linked their culture directly to the caribou: hunting the migrating herd for food, using their skins for clothing and shelter, and fashioning bone and antlers into tools and works of art. Much as limits to Maasai movement have affected their culture, recent plans for oil development in the calving grounds of the caribou could threaten and force permanent changes to this Inuit tradition. And as the Maasai focus on protecting the Serengeti ecosystem, the Arctic Inuit are taking a stand to promote the survival of the caribou.

Fewer lions hunt zebras and wildebeests today

Changes for Wildlife

THE GREAT MIGRATION still takes place in the Serengeti—wildebeests, in particular, still flood the plains in herds of over a million. But there is change here, too. One-third fewer lions now hunt the zebras and wildebeests. The once-astonishing populations of buffalos and giraffes have declined dramatically because their habitat has shrunk: large wheat farms now occupy land where the wild animals once lived. Poaching, especially of ivory, continues as a highly organized crime, despite international laws to control it, putting the elephant population at serious risk. Climate change means the rains aren't as predictable, and river levels are lower.

The Serengeti's Future

TIME IS CRITICAL to save this unique ecosystem and its endangered animals. International conservation organizations are using modern technology to collect information by satellite: for example, to make maps that can help track herds and show where poaching is happening. With quick access to this information, park ranger patrols can enforce the law better. Communities near park boundaries are being helped to grow food and keep livestock so they will no longer need to harvest wild animals. Knowledgeable local people, such as Maasai who work as guides and educators, help protect parks and the wildlife within them for everyone to experience. As long as future generations consider the needs of the ecosystem, herds will continue to answer the ancient call of migration on this unique route.

Wildebeests crossing the Mara River, along the Serengeti migration route

ROUTE 66

Highway to a New Life

NAME

Also known as Mother Road; Main
Street of America; Will Rogers
Highway; Dust Bowl Highway.

AGE

Construction of Route 66 began in 1926 and was completed in 1937. It took another year for the road to be fully paved. In the 1970s, modern interstate highways replaced most of the route. Its official life ended in 1984, when its signs were removed.

DESCRIPTION

Designed as a main east–west highway on a diagonal path across the U.S.: from Chicago through St. Louis, Tulsa, Oklahoma City, Amarillo, and Albuquerque, ending in Los Angeles.

CANADA

Chicago

St. Louis

Flagstaff

Los Angeles

Albuquerque

Amarillo

Tulsa

Oklahoma City

ATLANTIC OCEAN

GULF OF MEXICO

MEXICO

CLAIM TO FAME

Route 66 was seen as the road to opportunity for out-of-work Americans in the Great Depression and Dust Bowl years. It became a symbol of new optimism for young people after the Second World War. It also inspired motels, gas stations, roadside diners, drive-in movie theaters, books, songs, and even a TV series.

WHO USES IT NOW?

Historians studying 20th-century America, writers of guidebooks, and tourists curious to experience the road's mystique keep its memory alive. You can find and follow many short, original stretches, now marked with brown-and-white historic signs.

Erie, Pennsylvania
July 1947

Alice lugs another suitcase out to the car. She can see it won't fit in the trunk, already packed full with the family's bags and boxes. Did they really need to take so much stuff? The drive to the West Coast will take over two weeks on just one road, Route 66. They'll be staying at auto courts along the way. Mom says they'll see some famous places, like the Grand Canyon, as they pass through eight states. Alice thinks that part will be fun. But this packing business is not. It's so hot, all she wants to do is flop in the shade on the front porch. She drops the suitcase and gives it a kick. Let Dad worry about it. This is his idea, after all.

Alice couldn't believe it when her aunt and uncle from San Diego came for a visit and talked to her parents about moving west. Lots of good jobs, they said. She sees how that would appeal to her dad, who hasn't been able to get the kind of work he wants here. She knows he's anxious about money. Why, this car isn't even theirs. Her dad found a dealership looking for drivers to take new cars to Los Angeles, and he'll only have to buy the gas. It's too good a deal to pass up. But Alice isn't happy about leaving her friends and going to a new school if they decide to move—which they very well might. Her dad spent time out there in the navy during the war. He really liked it, said the winters were nice and warm.

Whatever Alice might think, it's too late to object any more. Her dad is locking the front door of their house. They are about to head west on the highway, and Alice has a strong feeling they won't be living here again.

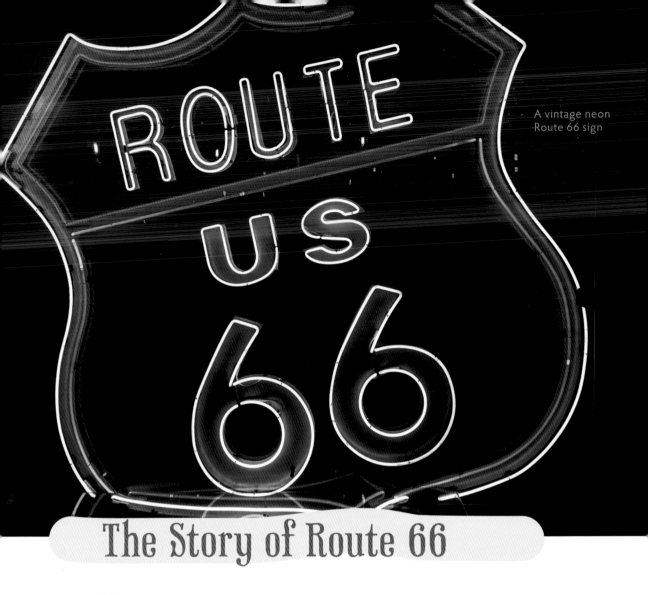

A vintage neon
Route 66 sign

The Story of Route 66

Take a look at a modern road map of the United States and you'll see a web of colored lines linking all its cities and towns. It's easy to find your way around. Major highways have solid lines. Dotted lines show gravel roads in rural areas. Almost all of the places on the map—marked with a large or small dot depending on population—can be reached on a numbered, paved road.

Yet only 100 years ago, things were different. In the early 1900s, a small number of paved roads connected only the largest cities. Other roads were unmarked footpaths or dirt wagon tracks—fine for short trips by horse and buggy. Why so few paved roads? Henry Ford only began producing the Model T in 1908, so not many Americans—about 500,000 in 1910—had automobiles. Most people traveled longer distances by railway, the cheapest and fastest way to get around and to deliver goods from place to place. As cars became more affordable, things changed rapidly. By 1920, car ownership had grown to 10 million. Obviously, more and better roads were needed.

One of the routes built during this time was an east–west highway named Route 66. Events in U.S. history following its construction shone a spotlight on this road, making it so popular that it eventually became a symbol of America's growth in the 20th century. What made Route 66 so important that it is still celebrated in story and song, long after being replaced by modern highways?

Early Trails Point the Way

EUROPEANS FIRST SETTLED in the eastern half of the U.S. As the population grew, they looked westward, seeking whatever riches the new territory had to offer. Explorers and those in search of gold and furs began to venture beyond the Mississippi River—a natural barrier between east and west. At first they followed hunting trails many aboriginals had used for centuries. In the 1800s, the Overland Trail took gold seekers to Northern California; the Oregon Trail led pioneers in covered wagons to the Pacific coast; and the Santa Fe Trail in New Mexico was a busy travel and trading road. These trails and others allowed settlers to penetrate the Western frontier before the first transcontinental railway was built in the 1860s. Parts of them later formed highways, like Route 66.

Pioneers heading west

Why Build this Highway?

As more and more people bought cars, the Federal Highway Act of 1921 provided money to state governments to build a system of highways. Years before, in 1916, Americans Cyrus Avery and John Woodruff had promoted the idea of a highway to link Chicago, Illinois, and Los Angeles, California. Avery's businesses included oil and coal mining, and selling land, all of which called for efficient transportation, and that depended on improved roads. The government's National Program of Highway and Road Development included a numbering system to make the roads easier to follow. Given the number "66" in 1926, Avery's new route would trace a diagonal line across the continent, through many small towns and rural communities that were far from existing main roads. The lack of roads had been a problem for farmers trying to move their grain and other agricultural produce to city markets—food that was needed for the growing population.

Beginning in 1926, Route 66 was built across stretches of flat prairie, farther south than other highways at the time. This meant travelers could avoid much of the stormy winter weather that made journeys hazardous on more northerly routes. With a faster all-season road, the number of trucks increased so quickly that by 1930, more goods were carried by road than railway.

In 1927 the National U.S. 66 Highway Association was created. One of its first tasks was to encourage each of the eight states the road would pass through to build their section and pave it as soon as possible. They named Route 66 "The Main Street of America" and advertised its benefits, as well as reporting on construction progress. One publicity idea, which some called a foolish stunt, was the First Annual Transcontinental Footrace from Los Angeles to Chicago, and on to New York. It was supposed to bring attention to the communities along Route 66. With a $25,000 prize to be awarded to the winner, a surprising 275 runners paid the hefty $100 entry fee (equal to over $1,300 U.S. today). The 1928 race was nicknamed the Bunion Derby: many of the runners who dropped out likely suffered sore feet! But after 87 days, 55 of the strongest reached New York. Top prize went to 20-year-old Andy Payne, an amateur runner in his first race, who was able to pay off his Oklahoma family's farm debts and whose name became part of the legend of Route 66.

TRAIL OF TEARS

The "Trail of Tears" was a tragic event in the history of the Cherokee people. In 1838, the Cherokee were ordered to leave their homeland in Georgia and resettle in Oklahoma (known then as Indian Territory), far from their traditional lands. The government wanted their land, and the gold discovered on it, for European immigrants. Although the Cherokee argued passionately against the removal, they were rounded up to begin a forced march. Families became separated, and those who left in summer suffered from a lack of water in the drought-plagued land. On the winter march, they struggled with cold, through muddy trails or ice-choked rivers, and with little food. About 4,000 people died, many from disease and hunger. Route 66 was later built on a short portion of this trail.

Hard Times in the 1930s

AFTER THE FIRST WORLD WAR, the economy in the United States was facing challenges. Many countries that struggled with massive debt looked to the wealthier young country for help to restore their economies, and that put a strain on resources. Then a stock market crash in 1929 hit Americans hard. The next decade saw high unemployment during a time called the Great Depression. And even worse was to come.

Up until the mid-1930s, farmers in the central and northern U.S. plains had been vigorously plowing their pastures and planting grain because prices had soared during the war years. But for several years, no rain fell in that region. The drought dried out the over-tilled land so badly that high winds easily lifted it into the sky, eventually blowing away an estimated 100 million acres of topsoil. After repeated dust storms, a horrific, rolling, dirt-filled cloud driven by powerful winds blotted out the sky over parts of

Route 66 through the Mojave Desert in California

Kansas, Oklahoma, and Texas on April 14, 1935—a day known as Black Sunday. People later described how the day turned so dark that chickens, thinking it was night, went to roost; how the winds pushed parked trucks far down the road; and how newly planted seeds were snatched right out of the ground. They saw dust driven into their homes through every tiny opening, and piles of it buried their fences, farm machinery, and their land, smothering their livelihoods. It became impossible to grow crops or to raise cattle, and finally more than half of the hungry population in "Dust Bowl" regions abandoned their farms in search of a better life. Many more whose farm-related jobs dried up like the thirsty land joined them—about 2.5 million in all.

Their escape to the West moved along the newly opened Route 66, which wove through their communities, giving the road its hopeful reputation as "the road to opportunity." Those travelers needed places to stay and meals, so dozens of small businesses sprang up along the way.

But unemployment still climbed. In an effort to get people working again, the government set up projects under a program called the New Deal. For example, thousands of out-of-work young men were given the job of paving the remaining sections of Route 66 all the way to California.

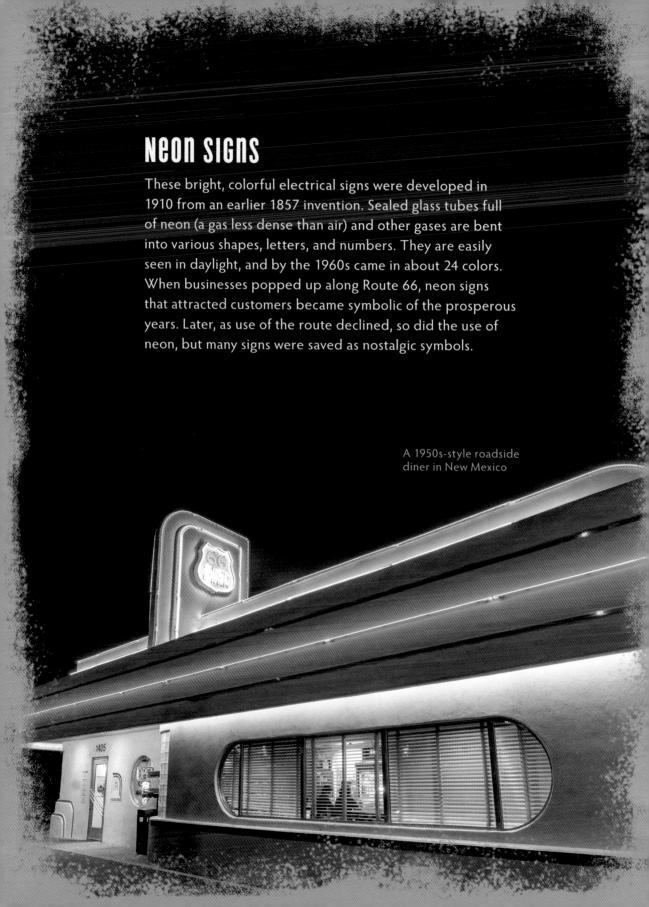

NEON SIGNS

These bright, colorful electrical signs were developed in 1910 from an earlier 1857 invention. Sealed glass tubes full of neon (a gas less dense than air) and other gases are bent into various shapes, letters, and numbers. They are easily seen in daylight, and by the 1960s came in about 24 colors. When businesses popped up along Route 66, neon signs that attracted customers became symbolic of the prosperous years. Later, as use of the route declined, so did the use of neon, but many signs were saved as nostalgic symbols.

A 1950s-style roadside diner in New Mexico

A War Road

THAT CONTINUOUS HARD SURFACE came just in time, in 1938, to meet the demands of the Second World War. In fact, half of the truck traffic along Route 66 had a military purpose: it was a key route to new bases for the armed forces, built in the wide-open spaces out West where the warm, dry climate was perfect for training exercises.

After the Japanese attacked Pearl Harbor, Hawaii, in 1941, officially drawing the United States into the war, the government took over the railway system to move equipment and soldiers to the Pacific coast. That left Route 66 as one of the most important highways for transporting steel, glass, and rubber in long truck convoys to production plants. In Detroit, car factories were converted to produce tanks, airplane engines, and transport vehicles for troops. Funds for new industries poured into California. And many of the 10 million people who crossed the country to fill these jobs created to support the war effort drove there on Route 66.

Its job wasn't done when the war ended, though. Now a peacetime highway, it welcomed the thousands of returning troops who bought cars once gas and tires were no longer rationed by war demands. Having enjoyed the comfortable climate in the Western states during their military training, many chose to settle there with their families. Along Route 66, large neon signs advertised the services that travelers needed: gas stations, motels, cafés, and restaurants. Small towns saw an economic boost. The 1950s and '60s were prosperous decades as people drove back and forth across the nation on business and for vacations. The highway became almost legendary: people wrote and sang about it, making it an even more popular part of the "American Dream" of wealth and success.

The End of "66"?

BUT THE ROAD'S GLORY DAYS were not to last much longer. Wartime use had taken its toll in wear and tear, and now the enormous increase in traffic showed up the weaknesses of the country's highway system. People no longer wanted to take their time along the old, narrow, two-lane roads, like Route 66. The Federal Aid Highway Act of 1956 provided funds for a new generation of fast, modern four-lane roads, called interstates, and soon drivers were dashing across the countryside at top speeds, pulling off briefly at rest areas rather than taking an exit to visit a town. It wasn't long before businesses in the small towns along the route began to close. Route 66 was actually replaced by five interstate highways. The last segment, in Arizona, was bypassed by an interstate in 1984, and all the official Route 66 signs were removed. The road that had helped America to

The route's end point at the Santa Monica pier

grow from a rough network of trails, that took it through decades of difficult economic times, and that saw huge populations shift from east to west, appeared to be lost in a new wave of historic changes.

It is still possible to trace the old highway by following the new ones (Route 66 often lies buried under the new pavement), looking for an unmarked access road, or a service road running beside the interstate or next to a railway line. But often there's only a dead-end stretch of pavement with weeds pushing through the cracks.

In spite of the modern need for speed, people won't let this symbolic road fade into memory. Wherever some of the old route still exists you'll find museums filled with early-model cars and trucks, and restored restaurants and diners using '50s and '60s themes and flashy neon signs as their decor. There's even a Route 66 Drive-In Theatre in Missouri, listed on the National Register of Historic Places. It operated from 1949 until the road lost its designation in 1985, but was later renovated and reopened in 1998. As one old song goes, you can still find some "kicks" on Route 66!

ROUTE 66 CELEBRATED

Songwriter Bobby Troup (1918–99) wrote "(GET YOUR KICKS ON) ROUTE 66" in 1946 during a road trip along the highway to California. The song became a hit when singer Nat King Cole (1919–65) recorded it.

Route 66 was nicknamed "THE WILL ROGERS HIGHWAY" to honor Will Rogers, Jr. (1879–1935), a performer, humorist, and journalist from Oklahoma remembered for his wise, down-to-earth observations about life.

John Steinbeck (1902–68) called it the "MOTHER ROAD" in his 1939 novel *The Grapes of Wrath*, about an Oklahoma family forced to move west during the Dust Bowl years.

The TV series **ROUTE 66** (1960–64) portrayed the adventures of two young men traveling across the U.S. in a Corvette, a classic car of the times.

HO CHI MINH TRAIL

Artery of War

NAME

Known in Vietnam as Truong Son Road, a name that comes
from the mountainous region the route passes through.
Its American nickname refers to President Ho Chi Minh
of North Vietnam. It is also nicknamed "Blood Road" for
the millions who died there during the Vietnam War.

AGE

After development began in 1959, it was expanded and maintained until 1975, then largely abandoned after the war. It was eventually replaced by the Ho Chi Minh Highway, begun in 2000.

DESCRIPTION

A maze of dirt tracks and waterways that connected isolated and sparsely populated communities, the trail was widened and in some places paved for all-season use. It ran from North Vietnam (Democratic Republic of Vietnam) to South Vietnam (Republic of Vietnam) mostly through the neighboring nations of Laos and Cambodia. The web of tracks was well hidden beneath jungle canopies in the rugged hillsides and forests of the western countryside.

CLAIM TO FAME

The Ho Chi Minh Trail became a critical supply route for North Vietnamese fighting American troops to gain control of South Vietnam in the 1960s and '70s. Tens of thousands of soldiers moved along the network of paths through mountain and jungle.

WHO USES IT NOW?

The paved Ho Chi Minh Highway that runs close to parts of the trail is used by commercial traffic, and is a popular motorcycle route for tourists.

NORTH VIETNAM

• Hanoi

Nape Pass

Mu Gia Pass

Ban Karai Pass

LAOS

THAILAND

Ho Chi Minh Trail

CAMBODIA

SOUTH VIETNAM

• Ho Chi Minh City (Saigon)

In the Vietnamese Mountains 1967

A deafening blast shakes the ground. It is quickly followed by another, and then more. Tuyen huddles on her mat, covering her ears and trembling. Each night, the bombing seems closer to the mountain cave where her family, along with dozens of others from their village, has sought shelter. Most nights it is impossible to sleep. Either the droning of low-flying American planes or the explosions along the jungle trail regularly destroy the silence. Tuyen remembers her home beside the rice paddies, where it was quiet enough to hear the nighttime music of crickets as she fell asleep. That life is gone now, and Tuyen fears she will never know it again.

Each morning her brothers go to help repair the trail, filling in the bomb craters to make it passable for supply trucks again. Tuyen will work the small terraced rice field it took so much effort to create on the hillside. The clearing is surrounded by branches—close enough that they can dash into the forest if planes approach. But it is not safe to stay in one place too long. They hope to harvest a small crop of rice before they must move farther south looking for new shelter and a place to farm. Tuyen's father struggles on his injured leg; he can't be a soldier now. But she is thankful his life was spared that dreadful day an enemy patrol caught them in the open. If it hadn't been for a group of their own People's Army hiding nearby, they would all be dead now.

Tuyen lies awake long after the attackers have moved on for the night. Will there ever again be a time when she isn't hungry, exhausted, and fearful, living this secretive and dangerous life? Her mother says it is best to think day by day. But Tuyen can't help imagining a time when this terrible war will end. It is the only hopeful thought that keeps her going.

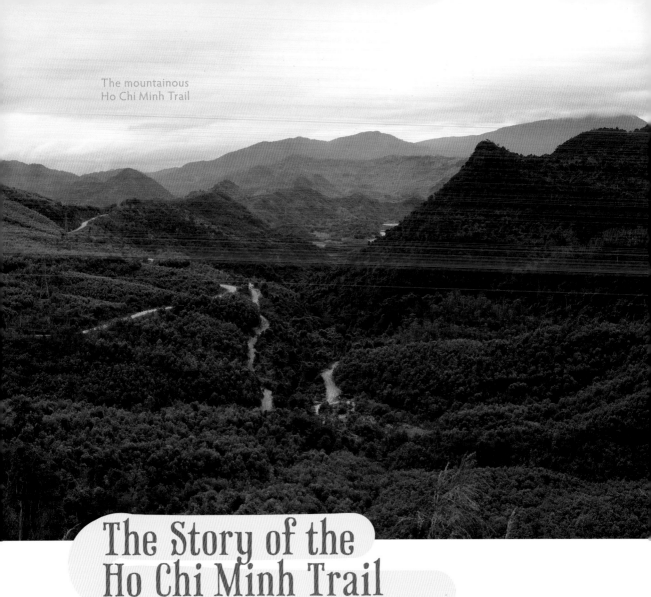

The mountainous
Ho Chi Minh Trail

The Story of the Ho Chi Minh Trail

Misty mountains and dense jungles form the western half of Vietnam, a narrow, S-shaped country in Southeast Asia. The rest is farmland, where the main agricultural crop, rice, grows in flooded fields called paddies. Some navigable rivers crisscross the land, which has a total area slightly smaller than New Mexico. Most of the 90 million people live near seaports or river deltas, on the eastern coastline. A main north–south highway along the coast links the largest cities, Hanoi and Ho Chi Minh City.

But another road takes travelers on a twisty route along the Annamese Mountains, which border the neighboring countries of Laos and Cambodia. Parts of the 3,185-kilometer (1,980-mile) Ho Chi Minh Highway shadow a historic route that has largely disappeared, overgrown once more by thick jungle. It was once a vital network of countless paths during a dark time in Vietnam's history.

Today, this increasingly industrial country enjoys one of the world's fastest-growing economies and is the second-largest exporter of rice and coffee—making it a dynamic land that offers a promising future for its people. It's hard to imagine that only 50 years ago, it was ravaged by war, parts of the land drenched in deadly chemicals. Why did the ancient Ho Chi Minh Trail become a major target in the 16-year-long Vietnam War?

Of Wars and Freedom

THE COUNTRYSIDE OF VIETNAM may look calm today, but throughout its history different foreign invaders have set out to conquer it. With China on its northern border, Vietnam was not surprisingly occupied by its giant neighbor for 1,000 years, beginning in the second century BCE. Already a major rice-growing area, it became a natural stopover for ships carrying trade between China and India. Following changes within dynasties that ruled China in the 10th century, Vietnam was able to regain its independence, and later it fought off Mongol aggressors under Kublai Khan.

In the 16th century, Portuguese traders sailed to Vietnam's shores and alerted other European countries to its agricultural resources. It became a colony of France in the mid-1800s until, during the Second World War, France itself was taken by Nazi Germany. Then Japan saw its chance to occupy Vietnam for a few years, keeping the last French-backed leader in place, until it withdrew following its defeat in the war. In the 1940s, a group called the Viet Minh, formed

by a revolutionary Communist leader named Ho Chi Minh, began to exert power in the north. Ho Chi Minh's goal was independence for the whole country, and his forces managed to finally defeat the French in 1954 in the First Indochina War. A postwar settlement split the country in two: North Vietnam went on under Communist rule, while an anti-Communist government remained in the south. This obstacle to Ho Chi Minh's wish for a united Vietnam foreshadowed more clashes.

During the Cold War of the 1960s, a time of political tension between the Soviet Union and the United States, the American government grew increasingly concerned about the spread of Communism. The Viet Cong (the name for Communist soldiers in North Vietnam) were waging a guerrilla-style war of sneak attacks against the south. The Ho Chi Minh Trail, built largely in secret, served as a link for a constant stream of military equipment and supplies, provided by North Vietnam's Soviet and Chinese allies.

In a fateful decision that would entangle them in a major struggle within a foreign country, the U.S. government decided to help the South Vietnamese repel supporters of the Communist Ho Chi Minh. From the arrival of the first American troops in 1965 until the U.S. accepted defeat and withdrew in 1975, the war pulled in over half a million U.S. soldiers. The United States had badly underestimated the strength and determination of North Vietnam to unify the country under Communist rule. Even though their aircraft dropped over eight million tons of bombs during the conflict, the Americans were never able to effectively control the flow of armies, weapons, and supplies through the jungle trails.

WAR'S LEFTOVERS

During the war, cluster bombs—containers filled with baseball-sized "bomblets"—scattered their deadly payload far and wide. But they didn't all blow up. An estimated 78 million of the small bombs dropped harmlessly onto rice paddies or in the middle of the jungle. Out of sight...but not always harmless. If not found by mine detectors, they are a constant threat as farmers work their fields. Over 100,000 people have lost arms or legs or been blinded when they accidentally disturbed one of these hidden hazards.

A model of a typical cluster bomb used in the Vietnam War

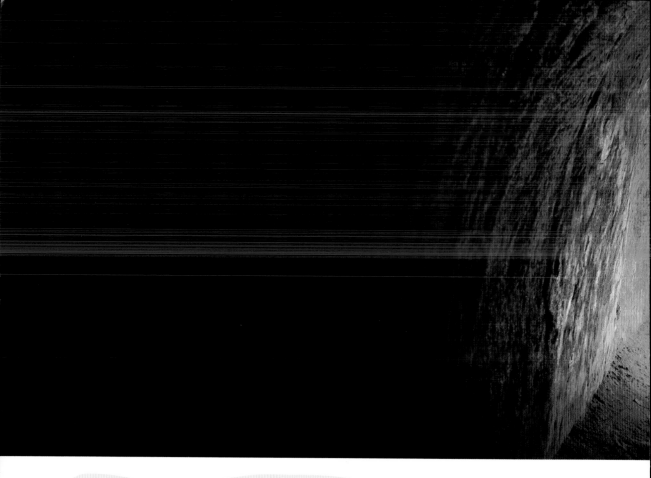

The Role of the Trail

LONG BEFORE THE HO CHI MINH TRAIL earned its name and wartime fame, local people used it to hunt tigers, or to move trade goods using elephants, ponies, bicycles, or simply by walking along ancient animal paths. Under a leafy canopy, the various tracks wound back and forth, sometimes crossing the borders of Vietnam's western neighbors, Laos and Cambodia. Typically, travel was slow, so before the Vietnam War it might have taken up to six months to move between the main centers of Hanoi in the north and Saigon (an earlier name for Ho Chi Minh City) in the south. Beginning in the 1950s, the Viet Minh used the route to ferry materials to the south to support Vietnam's fight for independence from French control. But the trail became a crucial weapon in the drawn-out 1960s conflict with the United States.

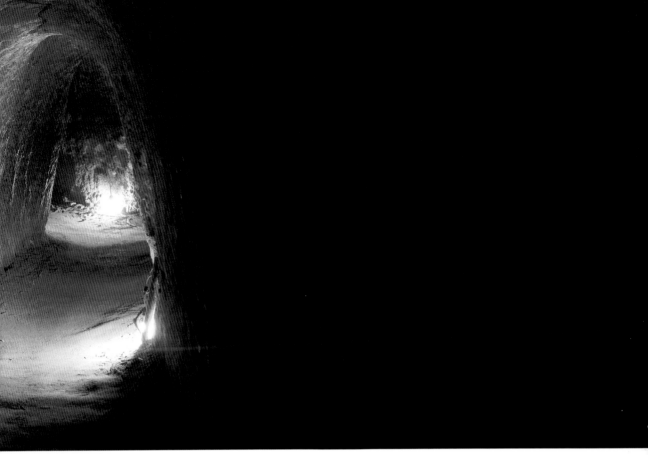

Inside the underground tunnels beneath Ho Chi Minh City

Dirt footpaths were widened into faster all-season roads, sometimes paved with stones to make them more functional in wet weather, suitable for trucks to move troops and equipment. All along the route, the North Vietnamese built command bases, storage facilities, camps, and small hospitals, much of this underground for safety from relentless bombing by the Americans. They dug tunnels big enough to hide hundreds of people from U.S. soldiers on the hunt for them. This transport and communication maze worked so well because it took place beneath natural cover that made detection difficult. The Vietnamese had the advantage of knowing the environment, being able to move stealthily at night and make expert use of camouflage by day. On the other hand, U.S. troops worked from permanent bases that were vulnerable to guerrilla attacks. Fighters sometimes posed as friendly villagers or farmers, and their intentions were impossible to predict or defend against.

Life in Wartime

THE WORST YEARS OF THE U.S. bombing campaign (between 1968 and 1972) completely disrupted the lives of Vietnam's civilian population. Many people had fled their homes and villages as the Americans set up their military bases, leaving rice fields—their livelihoods—to go hide in the mountains, often living in caves for years. They took up new farming practices, clearing patches of forest with fire to open areas for growing rice. If the smoke from these slash fires was thick enough, it sometimes disrupted the bombing. During the daytime, people wore dark, drab clothing instead of their customary bright colors so they would blend in with the ground and be less visible from aircraft. Working at night was safer.

Traditional terraced rice fields in Vietnam

But even so, a location might be used for only a single season before it became too dangerous.

Another challenge was to limit the amount of smoke produced while cooking food or heating a shelter, since fires might give away civilian locations to the enemy. During times when it was unsafe to cook, the Vietnamese existed on raw, wild foods. But many, especially children and the elderly, were unable to survive diseases like dysentery and malaria, and the lack of proper food and shelter. If they were injured or ill, people had to look after themselves unless they could reach a nearby field hospital. And if bombs fell nearby in the night, the villagers' first morning task would be to count up the lives lost. Often unable to recover bodies to bury, they had to abandon their cultural funeral customs. People lived in constant fear that the next bombing raid might wipe out their family.

Conquering the Trail

As THE WAR DRAGGED ON, the Ho Chi Minh Trail became more than just roads and pathways; ordinary Vietnamese people themselves became the most important part of the trail. In spite of the danger, determined local inhabitants continuously cleared and repaired the roads pitted by bombs to keep supplies moving for their troops. This allowed them to support their fighters with shelter that could be moved when necessary, and with information about enemy activity in the area. They helped by planting land mines to slow the movement of U.S. soldiers on the trails. Then they worked feverishly overnight to repair craters caused by the explosions. They pitched in to build bridges that lay just beneath the surface of rivers, so U.S. aircraft couldn't see them. By the end of the war, the trail even had truck-repair and refueling stops, and anti-aircraft positions to defend it. Now the journey from north to south could be made in only a week.

The Americans, at a disadvantage in the unfamiliar jungle terrain, believed they had to cut off the Ho Chi Minh Trail if they wanted to stop the Communist takeover of the south. An invisible enemy was impossible to fight effectively, so the U.S. tried to even the odds. They dropped electronic sensors that would pick up any movement on the trail. They used bulldozers to plow up the vegetation, and chemical sprays (about 75 million liters, or 20 million gallons) to kill it. One of these chemicals was called Agent Orange, for the color identifying its containers. From helicopters and other aircraft, this herbicide, containing highly poisonous dioxin, was sprayed in far greater amounts and with a much stronger mix than intended for its original use—to control weeds in agriculture. In fact, one of its ingredients was later banned for use in the U.S. The Americans reasoned that a jungle without leaves would hide little, exposing the pathways and enemy bases and wiping out food crops the Vietnamese army depended on. Of course, that was also the food source for civilians, and its loss led to widespread starvation. Used along trails and waterways, the dioxin in Agent Orange killed every plant it touched—but it landed on people as well.

As a result, another menacing effect has been seen in the years since the war. Research is still ongoing, but dioxin is believed to be responsible for hundreds of thousands of birth defects and illnesses in the people who came in contact with it—perhaps over four million, both Vietnamese and Americans. After the war, empty herbicide containers were often simply rinsed out and used in various ways by local merchants. Dioxin's deadly effects still linger in the soil throughout the sprayed areas, and it shows up in the food chain—for instance, in ducks and fish that are eaten by people. In 2012, the U.S. began work to help clean up some contaminated sites in Vietnam.

When it appeared that American troops were unable to conquer and hold territory—the usual way a military force takes control—their focus turned to reducing the numbers of the enemy. One method was another devastating weapon: napalm, a mixture of explosives. It was first used in flamethrowers to clear jungle vegetation where enemy fighters might hide, but it was later also dropped in bombs. It burns at super-hot temperatures as it clings to the skin, and most victims—many of them civilians—died in extreme pain. Even in the face of such horrific weapons as Agent Orange and napalm, the Vietnamese persisted in defending their land.

A U.S. helicopter spraying the dense Vietnamese jungle in 1969

RESTORING THE ENVIRONMENT

War destroys not only people and economies, but also the natural environment. Forest and farmland demolished during the Vietnam War equaled an area about three times the size of the state of Delaware. Without the leafy cover to protect it, jungle soil was pounded by the region's seasonally heavy rains, which eroded it and washed out nutrients. Lower humidity levels and temperatures, kept high before by the jungle canopy, changed the habitat of birds, insects, tree-dwelling mammals, and reptiles. Since the war, a small fraction of the species that used to inhabit the area still remains.

The country's bombed and burned hillsides are now being replanted with a variety of greenery. From pepper plants and rubber trees to acacia—a fast-growing tree—life is being restored to the land.

A Vietnamese farmer tending peach trees in 2015

Losers ... and Winners

AMERICAN LOSSES BEGAN TO ADD UP as well, and not just in casualties. Back home in the United States, people were shocked by the terrible images of war along the Ho Chi Minh Trail shown on television. News of mass killings of civilians stirred up protests and launched antiwar marches. The economy began to feel the negative effects of the huge wartime investment overseas. When the U.S. finally pulled out of Vietnam, over 58,000 American soldiers had died. The death count of Vietnamese was over 4.8 million, and that country's economy had been destroyed.

In 1976, the Communist government declared victory for the United Socialist Republic of Vietnam, and the largest southern city, Saigon, was renamed Ho Chi Minh City. Rather than suffer ruthless treatment under their new rulers, many South Vietnamese escaped in small boats as desperate refugees. Often the overloaded boats sank far from shore.

The jungle pathways and people of the Ho Chi Minh Trail had played a crucial part in bringing about a victory, but at an extremely high price for all.

A BRIGHTER FUTURE

Vietnam is still under the rule of Communism—a system in which the state owns all property, factories, farms, and resources and controls workers' earnings. But starting in the 1990s, the country relaxed its rules to allow private companies and individuals to do business there. This economic move has helped reduce poverty, attract investment from foreign countries, and encourage tourism. The United States is no longer seen as an enemy, and now buys many goods from Vietnam.

Conclusion

THE PEOPLE CAUGHT UP IN historic events along these
10 important routes, scattered across the Earth and through the
centuries, have given us a wider understanding of today's world.
Through their stories, we can relive their experiences from long
ago, try to imagine what they saw, and trace the effects of their
decisions and actions. We can admire the courage and strength
of the earliest inhabitants in a frigid northern land. We can
marvel at the skill of those who created roads and railways
without today's powerful technologies. We can understand the
determination to complete difficult journeys with high hopes,
and to stand up for beliefs. Valuable lessons unfolded on each
of these paths.

What new land routes have yet to be discovered? And what
new knowledge might yet be found? People continue to explore
remote and challenging places on Earth—descending into the
deepest caves, crossing inhospitable landscapes at the North and
South Poles, penetrating the mysterious tangle of rainforests.
They compete to be the first to hike or bike across continents.
Each journey leads to new awareness about oneself, or something
that might help another. Each step along the route writes the
stories that will remain for others to discover.

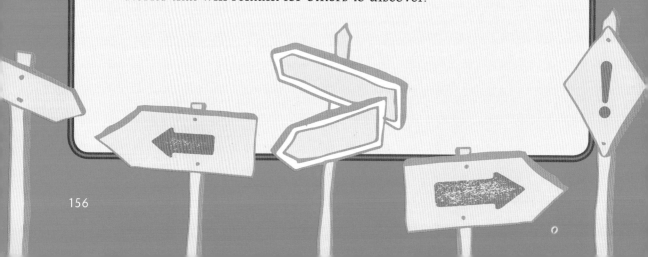

Selected Bibliography

Adney, Tappen. *Klondike Stampede.* New York: Harper & Brothers, 1900.

Andrews, Phil, and Phil Harding. "Following the Fosse Way through Nottinghamshire: Archaeology and the A46." Cotswold Wessex Archaeology, 2012. Retrieved from the Highways England website. highways.gov.uk/publications/a46-newark-to-widmerpool-improvement-following-the-fosse-way-through-nottinghamshire-archaeology-and-the-a46/.

Antonson, Rick. *Route 66 Still Kicks: Driving America's Main Street.* Toronto: Dundurn, 2012.

Bauer, Brian S. "Suspension Bridges of the Inca Empire." *Andean Archaeology III,* edited by Helaine Silverman and William H. Isbell, 468–93. New York: Springer, 2006. academia.edu/6953894/Suspension_Bridges_of_the_Inca_Empire.

Blumenthal, Ralph. "Protection Sought for Vast and Ancient Incan Road." *New York Times,* June 18, 2014. nytimes.com/2014/06/19/arts/design/protection-sought-for-vast-and-ancient-incan-road.html?_r=1.

Brierly, John. *A Pilgrim's Guide to the Camino de Santiago.* Forres, Scotland: Camino Guides, 2003.

de la Bédoyère, Guy. *Roman Britain.* New York: Thames & Hudson, 2006.

Docherty, Paddy. *The Khyber Pass: History of Empire and Invasion.* New York: Faber & Faber, 2007.

Elias, Scott. "Bridge to the Past." *Earth* 6, issue 2 (Apr. 1997): 51.

Fagan, Brian. *The First North Americans: An Archaeological Journey.* London: Thames & Hudson, 2011.

GlobalSecurity.org. "Ho Chi Minh Trail." globalsecurity.org/military/world/vietnam/ho-chi-minh-trail.htm.

Goldman, Mara J. "Strangers in Their Own Land: Maasai and Wildlife Conservation in Northern Tanzania." *Conservation & Society* 9, issue 1 (2011): 65–79. doi: 10.4103/0972-4923.79194.

Heale, Jay. *Cultures of the World: Tanzania.* New York: Marshall Cavendish Benchmark, 2010.

Ibeji, Dr. Mike. "An Overview of Roman Britain." BBC online, Feb. 17, 2011. bbc.co.uk/history/ancient/romans/questions_01.shtml.

Knowles, Drew. *Route 66 Adventure Handbook.* Solana Beach, CA: Santa Monica Press, 2011.

Lamb, David. "Revolutionary Road." *Smithsonian,* Mar. 2008, 56–66. smithsonianmag.com/travel/revolutionary-road-21003988/?no-ist.

Loxterkamp, David. "The Road to Compostela." *Commonweal* 131, issue 4 (Feb. 27, 2004).

Maasai Association. maasai-association.org/lion.html.

MacQuarrie, Kim. *Last Days of the Inca.* New York: Simon & Schuster, 2007.

Mattingly, David. *An Imperial Possession: Britain in the Roman Empire.* London: Penguin, 2006.

Meltzer, David J. *First Peoples in a New World: Colonizing Ice Age America.* Berkeley: University of California Press, 2009.

National Historic Route 66 Federation. "History of Route 66." national66.org/resources/history-of-route-66/.

Neufeld, David, and Frank Norris. *Chilkoot Trail: Heritage Route to the Klondike.* Madeira Park, BC: Harbour Publishing, 1996.

Ochsendorf, John. "Inka Engineering Symposium 4: Suspension Bridge Technology." Smithsonian NMAI video, Nov. 2013.

Payne, Adam A., and Douglas A. Hurt. "Narratives of the Mother Road: Geographic Themes Along Route 66." *Geographical Review* 105, issue 3 (Jul, 2015): 283–303. doi: 10.1111/j.1931-0846.2015.12074.x.

Pholsena, Vatthana. "Life under Bombing in Southeastern Laos (1964–1973) Through the Accounts of Survivors in Sepon." *European Journal of East Asian Studies* 9, issue 2 (Dec. 2010): 267–290. doi: 10.1163/156805810X548766.

Pringle, Heather. "The First Americans." *Scientific American*, Nov. 2011, 36–45. scientific american.com/article/first-americans-researchers-reconsider-peopling-new-world/.

Schofield, Victoria. *Afghan Frontier: At the Crossroads of Conflict.* New York: Tauris Parke Paperbacks, 2010.

Shape, William. *Faith of Fools: A Journal of the Klondike Gold Rush.* Pullman, WA: Washington State University Press, 1998.

Slepnev, Igor. "The Trans-Siberian Railway." *History Today* 46, no. 11 (Nov. 1996): 37–39.

Stewart, Jules. "A Passage to Pakistan." *Geographical* 77, no. 6 (June 2005): 30–36.

Thomas, Bryn. *Trans-Siberian Handbook.* Surrey, UK: Trailblazer Publications, 2011.

US History.com. "Ho Chi Minh Trail." u-s-history.com/pages/h1875.html.

Wolmar, Christian. *To the Edge of the World: The Story of the Trans-Siberian Express, the World's Greatest Railroad.* New York: PublicAffairs, 2013.

Yukon Archives. "Klondike Goldrush." tc.gov.yk.ca/archives/klondike/en/prologue.html.

Zoellner, Thomas. *Trains: Riding the Rails That Created the Modern World—from the Trans-Siberian to the Southwest Chief.* New York: Viking, 2014.

Further Reading

Booth, David. *The Dust Bowl.* Toronto: Kids Can Press, 1996.

Butterfield, Moira. *The Romans in Britain.* New York: Franklin Watts, 2010.

Ellis, Deborah. *Mud City.* Toronto: Groundwood, 2003.

Greenwood, Barbara. *Gold Rush Fever: A Story of the Klondike, 1898.* Toronto: Kids Can Press, 2001.

Gregory, Kristiana. *Seeds of Hope: The Gold Rush Diary of Susanna Fairchild, California Territory, 1849.* New York: Scholastic, 2001.

Gruber, Beth. *Ancient Inca: Archaeology Unlocks the Secrets of the Inca's Past.* Washington, DC: National Geographic, 2007.

Heuer, Karsten. *Being Caribou.* New York: Walker, 2007.

Khamala, M. M. *Summer of Leopard Maasai.* CreateSpace, 2009.

Lauber, Particia. *Who Came First? New Clues to Prehistoric Americans.* New York: National Geographic, 2003.

Murphy, Claire Rudolf. *Children of the Gold Rush.* Boulder, CO: Roberts Rinehart, 1999.

Pole, Graeme. *Great Railways of the Canadian West.* Canmore, AB: Altitude Publishing, 2006.

Richardson, Gillian. *Machu Picchu.* Calgary: Weigl, 2009.

Rockefeller, Laurel A. *Boudicca: Britain's Queen of the Iceni.* Laurel Rockefeller, 2014.

Rubalcaba, Jill. *Every Bone Tells a Story: Hominid Discoveries, Deductions and Debates.* Watertown, MA: Charlesbridge, 2010.

Skrypuch, Marsha Forchuk. *Last Airlift: A Vietnamese Orphan's Rescue from War.* Toronto: Pajama Press, 2011.

Whelan, Gloria. *Goodbye, Vietnam.* New York: Yearling, 1993.

Image Credits

Index

ABOUT THE AUTHOR

Gillian Richardson worked as a teacher-librarian before she began writing her own books. She has been fascinated by maps since childhood, when she would listen to her dad's stories about his sea voyages and find his destinations in a world atlas. So she was pleased that her research for this book included studying maps of each route.

Gillian has had the good fortune to live in and explore several Canadian provinces. Beyond Canada, maps have led her along some Roman roads in Britain and on highways that cross parts of U.S. Route 66. When she's closer to her home, on Shuswap Lake in British Columbia, she enjoys hiking a network of nearby nature trails.

Two of Gillian's previous books with Annick Press—*Kaboom! Explosions of All Kinds* and *10 Plants That Shook the World*—are award winners.

ABOUT THE ILLUSTRATOR

Kim Rosen was raised in a suburb of Philadelphia, Pennsylvania, and could usually be found in her room quietly drawing pictures. Kim studied advertising design at the Fashion Institute of Technology in New York City. She worked as a designer for several years, then realized she was meant to be an illustrator, and moved to Georgia to attend the Savannah College of Art and Design, where she earned an MFA in illustration.

Today Kim lives with her partner in Northampton, Massachusetts, and works out of her studio in an old factory building overlooking the mountains in nearby Easthampton. She has illustrated for magazines (*The New Yorker*, *The Atlantic*), newspapers (*The Boston Globe*, *The Globe and Mail*) and corporate clients (Billabong, Starbucks, American Express). She illustrated the three previous books in the World of Tens series.